Thinking of...

Building a Microsoft Cloud Operating Model?

Ask the Smart Questions

By Dan Scarfe, Sean Morris, Frank
Bennett and Ray Bricknell

First Published in 2018 by Smart Questions Limited, Fryern House, 125 Winchester Road, Chandlers Ford, Hampshire, SO53 2DR, UK
Web: *www.smart-questions.com* (including ordering of printed and electronic copies, extended book information, community contributions and details on charity donations)
Email: *info@smart-questions.com* (for customer services, bulk order enquiries, reproduction requests et al)

A catalogue record for this book is available from the British Library.

ISBN 978-1-907453-23-6

SQ-23-194-001-001

Smart Questions™ Philosophy

Smart Questions is built on 3 key pillars, which set it apart from other publishers:

1. *Smart people want Smart Questions not Dumb Answers*
2. *Domain experts are often excluded from authorship, so we are making writing a book simple and painless*
3. *The community has a great deal to contribute to enhance the content*

www.smart-questions.com

Reviews

Clare Barclay

Chief Operating Officer, Microsoft UK

"Building a Microsoft Cloud Operating Model is a must read for leaders looking to understand how the rules of the game have changed, and importantly how to unlock the value that comes with the right model, great technologies and engaged people.

I love the fact it's practical and serves as a useful guide for those driving change and innovation in their business."

Dr Richard Sykes

Chairman, Cloud industry Forum

"In the early 1990s I was asked to build on two decades of international business management experience to take on a global IT leadership role – my brief was to draw on my business insight to transform the work of a very techie inheritance. Twenty five years on, well into the era of 'the cloud', this challenge still remains, alas, across much of our industry.

The title 'Building a Microsoft Cloud Operating Model' suggests a technical agenda, but in reality the four authors draw on their wide experience to provide the means for business (CXO) leadership (who should read this book) to bring themselves into effective partnership with their IT (CIO) colleagues at a crucial time – and vice versa!

This blending is genuinely vital now that so much powerful new technology - and Cloud-rooted capabilities, such as AI, are transforming how business can and will be done. The chapter on Agile in particular is an excellent read!"

Author(s)

Dan Scarfe

Dan is a passionate technologist and loves imagining the impact that technology can have on every aspect of people's lives. As Founder of New Signature UK, Dan heads up the Solutions team. New Signature helps enterprise organisations harness the power of the Microsoft cloud.

He helps conceive new products and services which can help organisations digitally differentiate, working closely with the sales and delivery teams. Dan is also part of the global products and GTM teams.

Dan has been deeply engaged with Microsoft's cloud since its inception in 2008. He was advising Microsoft on Azure when it was still called Red Dog and has seen the platform evolve substantially over that time. He presents on this topic around the world and sits on two Microsoft Partner Advisory Councils. Dan is also actively involved in the community, sitting on another two Microsoft Partner Association boards.

Dan has been involved in many start-ups over the years, some successful, some not, and does his bit through passing on lessons learned as a mentor within Microsoft for Start-ups.

Dan has authored one other book in the Smart Questions series.

Frank Bennett FRSA

Frank has a long career in Information Technology from the forgotten age of the mainframe and every evolution preceding the cloud era.

He was on the leadership team of a Microsoft Gold Partner then recognised as a pioneer of cloud computing at Microsoft WPC 2007.

Later he went on to write books distributed by Microsoft at WPC and made available as a download from Microsoft Partner Portal. He is mentor to Microsoft ScaleUp London. More recently he was an independent expert advising the EU Horizon 2020 CloudWatch2 program from which he is attributed as the inventor of Market Readiness Levels and their conjoining with Technology Readiness levels.

Now with a portfolio career he holds the Financial Times Non-Executive Director Diploma and is qualified to advise on General Data Protection Regulation (GDPR) following completion of the GDPR Transition Programme at the world-renowned Henley Business School. He is Deputy Chair of the UK Cloud Industry Forum and a Director of the Federation Against Software Theft.

A Fellow of the RSA, Member of the Institute of Directors, Member of EY Independent Director Programme and the ICSA:Governance Institute.

Frank has authored eight books in the Smart Questions series.

Ray Bricknell

With 37 years of international IT experience, Australian entrepreneur Ray Bricknell has been actively facilitating and commenting on the relationship between the mid-tier UK Financial Services sector and the UK Cloud Vendor community since 2010.

Ray's firm Behind Every Cloud developed the award winning and industry accredited Clover (Cloud Vendor Ratings) index. He provides advisory services to a diverse range of large and small clients from the Asset Management/Investment Management/ Hedge, Private Equity, Retail, Investment and Private Banking and Insurance. Formerly the CTO of an $8Bn listed Hedge Fund. Ray is currently Chair of the Cloud Industry Forum Financial Services Special Interest Group.

Sean Morris

Sean has been involved in the IT industry since the early 90s and has sat on both sides of the consultancy world as an in-house IT staffer and a consultant working for large systems integrators.

Sean has a background in professional services from working as part of an IT team for a top London based law firm and in Telco working in Australia. Sean specialises in infrastructure services particularly around hosting and service management.

Sean runs a team of cloud advisors and pre-sales consultants for New Signature UK pretending he works for Dan.

Sean is passionate about the business of IT and the role IT can play in contributing to the success of organisations.

Table of Contents

Volume 1
'What the leadership team need to know'

1 The Digital Age 1

2 The Digital Wave 7

3 The Way Ahead 17

4 The Race is on 23

5 Agile – small word quick work 33

6 The Business Questions 41

Volume 2
'What the technical team need to know'

7 A new operating model 73

8 Strategy and service providers 77

9 Procurement and financial governance 89

10 Service management 97

11 Access control, security and provisioning 109

12 Monitoring, management and automation 125

13 DevOps and application development 133

14 The Technical Questions 149

Closing thoughts

15 Funny you should say that 185

16 Final Word 191

Acknowledgements

We'd like to offer huge thanks to everyone that has helped and supported us as we wrote this book. The list is too long to thank each person, but particular thanks to:

- Mark Smith for championing this initiative inside Microsoft and encouraging us to do this.
- Steve Bryant-Brown and Stelios Zarras for your help and support along the way.
- John Kendrick for sharing his valuable insights in the first story at the end of the book.
- Pete Gatt from Vibrato who contributed a huge amount to the thought around some of the concepts we describe, along with helping to write a good chunk of the book and sharing the second story at the end of the book.
- New Signature for giving us the time to write this book.
- Jane Scarfe for proof reading.
- Lara Scarfe for letting Dan spend endless evenings and weekends writing.

Foreword

Mark Smith, Senior Director

Azure + AI, Microsoft

We live in a time of unprecedented change. Digital and broader technology innovation are reshaping our world all around us.

The introduction of the cloud and on-demand access to computing power far in excess of anything available to organisations before have turbo-charged this already fast rate of innovation and change.

In recent years, the cloud has evolved from a set of technologies that augment mission-critical platforms, to become that mission-critical platform. It is no longer something used for lower impact workloads. It is becoming the central platform organisations are leveraging as the lynchpin of their digital transformation strategies.

As we hurtle along on this journey of change, it's sometimes difficult to give ourselves the time to take stock. To take the time to look back on what we have achieved. To assess what has worked and what requires more effort. To learn from others about their successes and failures. To understand and evaluate what good looks like.

This book seeks to do just this.

Embracing cloud in your organisation is more than just moving servers from on premises to someone else's datacentre. That part is the easy part. Fully embracing cloud necessitates taking a long, hard look at your organisation. What does digital mean to you? How do you go about digitally transforming your organisation? What aspects of technology can you embrace to allow you to not only survive but also thrive in this brave new world?

This conversation extends far beyond the remit of your IT department. As leaders within your business, simply delegating the problem to IT is not the answer. Technology in itself is not the answer. The answer falls exactly between the traditional realms of business and IT. To truly digitally transform your organisation your business leaders need to understand the role technology can play and imagine new technology-powered products and services. At the same time, your technology leaders need to far more closely align themselves with the business. It is these teams and these individuals who are uniquely placed to transform these ideas into reality.

The key to digital transformation is to seamlessly blend what we might describe as a business operating model with our traditional IT operating model. Only when these teams and these concepts truly combine can we be successful in this brave new world.

This book argues the need to establish a cloud operating model as this unique bridge between these two, separate worlds. A seamless combination of business and IT operating models.

A combination of these two completely separate worlds is, however, fraught with difficulty.

The primary currency of a business operating model is agility. Business owners and business group leaders thirst this agility. They are often perplexed as to why things are perceived as being so difficult and time consuming. They are focussed on customers and delivering them the capabilities they desire. Everything that gets in the way of this is unnecessary complexity and roadblocks.

The primary focus of an IT operating model is control. IT leaders wake at night worrying about availability, security and a raft of factors completely alien to the business. IT often shies away from innovation and change as it is often in direct competition with their driving goals.

This mismatch is one of the primary contributors to the "shadow IT" phenomenon of recent years. Business leaders demanding a level of agility not being adequately delivered by the IT department simply pull out their corporate credit cards and procure what they need, then and there.

Uncontrolled and unabated procurement of IT solutions is not a good long-term strategy. Control is still a necessity within larger, structured organisations.

A cloud operating model as described within this book seeks to achieve the best of both worlds. The agility demanded by the business with the control needed by the IT teams.

Who should read this book?

This book is presented in two volumes.

- Volume 1 is for the non-technical reader, those concerned with shaping the organisation.
- Volume 2 is for the learned technical reader, those concerned with solving how technology supports the organisation.

We encourage readers to read both volumes so when non-technical and technical audiences come together there is a mutual understanding of what is on the mind of the other.

This book is about a Cloud Operating Model and what we mean by that is how your organisation consumes the resources of public cloud-based services to compete in this digital age. In chapter 15 "Funny you should say that", we have invited people who have got the T-shirt to put that in their own words.

People like you and me

This book is aimed squarely at those who want to effect a change in the way IT services and specifically cloud services are consumed and delivered to an organisation. Those that recognise the vital role IT plays in a world that is increasingly technology driven in what is commonly referred to as the 'digital age'. Those that want to become change agents. People like you and me.

This book is intended to be a catalyst for action aimed at a range of people inside and outside your organisation. Here are just a few, and why it is relevant to them.

The Board

At one time IBM was king of computing and spread FUD (Fear Uncertainty and Doubt) and that it would be foolish to consider any other choice. Let us offer a new Three Letter Acronym, MUD (More Uncertainty and Doubt), as technology weighs heavy on the strategy of the business and the impact of making a bad or ill-considered decision.

The board has many things to consider and technology has bounced up the agenda with pundits remarking every business is now a digital business. With the rate of technological innovation and the pervasive use of cloud computing it is a juggling act to 'not get left behind' never mind 'get ahead'.

This book describes a model for how a business will combine technology (the legacy IT with the innovation of cloud computing) to deal with complexity of the ever-increasing reliance on technology. Don't be fearful that you will drown in techno-speak as the book is in two volumes; volume 1 talks about and sets questions you will want to ask of yourself and others to know what organisational capability needs to exist to support the business strategy.

There is an emerging techno-political debate that places a new responsibility on organisations in respect of the processing of data. This is attracting the attention of the media and is a hot debate. A legal responsibility and accountability now accompany the decision to invest in technology such as Artificial Intelligence for the processing of data, and in some jurisdictions like the European Union the consequences of non-compliance are severe.

The CxO team

Information Technology in the past was for boffins. That all changed over the last two decades and now everyone is expected to be computer savvy. It is hard to imagine a discussion involving the CxO team that does not include technology. The thing is, it is getting an ever more complex discussion as 'business' and 'technology' are interwoven and core to business strategy and execution. Management has the ultimate responsibility for business outcomes and today's leaders must operate in the style of leaner ways of thinking and operating, as revealed in this book.

A measure of a successful company is how it is harnessing technology and how that is both an offensive and defensive strategy in a world that has a long list of established businesses going from glory to bust and the 'oh poor them' analysis of what happened. We all know who they are, we used to shop there, they were a supplier and so on.

So, if technology is now "make or break" then this book is for you to engage the Board and Line of Business Managers in a discussion about 'what the business has to be good at', whether that is customer service, optimisation of the supply chain or supporting a mobile workforce to name a few. These things describe how the business operates and this book serves up a discussion about how that evolves with technology and harnessing the power and innovation of cloud computing. The execution of that does not happen without the IT team in tow.

Line of Business Manager

There is no better place to understand the demands of the business than those at the sharp end. You may hear your competitors are delivering new products and services more quickly or making it easier and more convenient for customers to conduct their day-to-day business. The availability of cloud computing has created new opportunities for LOB managers to respond quickly and equip their teams with new ways to deliver productivity and work smart. That has served its purpose well and is now part of the big picture of how the business will create an agile posture to the deployment of technology.

CIO / CTO

The CIO and CTO are key architects of the transformation we describe in this book and your role will fundamentally change. You're going to move from expert execution to expert execution plus leading transformation. The cloud operating model is your strategic answer to this change in role.

IT Manager

Depending on the size of the organisation, you as IT Manager will take the lead as you are where the rubber meets the road. Where strategy meets execution and reality. You'll be the chief architect of this new cloud operating model and this book will equip you with everything you need to build it.

How to use this book

This book is intended to be the catalyst for action. We hope that the ideas and examples inspire you to act. So, do whatever you need to do to make this book useful. Go to our website and email colleagues the e-book summary. Use Post-it notes, write on it, rip it apart, or read it quickly in one sitting. Whatever works for you. We hope this becomes your most dog-eared book.

Smart Questions

At the end of each volume you will see a table of questions. Not all the questions will necessarily be new or insightful. The value you get from the information will clearly vary. It depends on your job role and previous experience. We call this the 3Rs.

The 3 Rs

Some of the questions will be in areas where you know the answers already, so the questions will **Reinforce** them in your mind.

You may have forgotten some aspects of the subject, so the questions will **Remind** you.

Other questions may **Reveal** new insights to you that you've never considered before.

We trust that you will find real insights. There may be some "aha" moments. In this context, probably the most critical role of the Smart Questions is to reveal risks that you might not have considered. On the flip side they should also open up your thinking to opportunities that hadn't yet occurred to you. Balancing the opportunities and the risks, and then agreeing what is realistically achievable is the key to formulating an effective strategy.

The questions could be used in your internal operational meetings to inform the debate. Alternatively, they could shape the discussion you have with your IT vendors and their partners.

Visit *www.cloudoperatingmodel.com* for even more content and information.

Building a Microsoft Cloud Operating Model

'What the leadership team need to know'

Chapter

1

The Digital Age

Someone is sitting in the shade today because someone planted a tree a long time ago

Warren Buffett (Businessman, 1930-)

A new dawn

A ROUND the world the disruptive promises of the infamous dot com bubble of the late nineties and early noughties are finally being realised. The current generation of IT that had cloud enter everyday vocabulary has businesses embracing digital transformation and digital enabled business methods. As a result, a new requirement has emerged for a different kind of Operating Model – a Cloud Operating Model (**COM**). As we will explain, the Cloud Operating Model is the new lingua franca for the business and IT teams to communicate and collaborate and get down to work. The digital agenda is commanding CEO attention worldwide, and its outcomes will set the scene for high-speed business change over the next decade.

The balance between *agility* and *control* is a key theme in this book, and we will advocate the necessity of (some) sacrifice of *control* in order to enable the *agility* now demanded by a business competing in a digital world. Moving the dial toward *agility* is set to challenge IT teams and that is also explored in this book.

A new day, a new way

One of the unforeseen side effects with the adoption of cloud is 'shadow IT' - a term used to describe infrastructure and applications purchased or developed by the business without the engagement of the IT department. Why did that happen? Quite simply the cloud served up new ways for business teams to get things done fast without the need to be (or engage) technologists. Shadow IT supports line of business to move fast, with full *control*, and *agility* to do what they need to do. It is also accounted for within delegated budgets and treated as an expense rather than an asset and some say has resulted in a loss of control of all-up IT expenditure and with-it governance, standardisation, economies of scale and overall strategic coordination suffer. Ho hum, things are getting done and that's what matters most. Right?

New horizons

The prevailing 'best practice' for centralised IT/business oversight is the formality of the 'IT Operating Model' (ITOM) as an aid to communication, coordination and *control,* and intermediary roles and translation functions like IT Project Managers and Business Analysts exist to define and agree:

- The requirements and priorities of the business
- The objectives and constraints before work starts
- The budget and forecast future spend
- Formal plans and reporting for transition and migration
- Structured processes to align the goals and work, such as Waterfall and Prince 2 etc. Check out the Appendix for a definition.

The ITOM model can frustrate business teams' projects in a queue of corporate priorities that are seemingly in time perpetually delayed. If they want results now they are tempted by the shadow IT option. The prevailing ITOM and Business Operating Model (BOM) pairing is not equipped to deal with this new cloud phenomenon - end user power.

Shadow IT costs continue to skyrocket, creating data silos and system duplication in some cases. Yet still, it is no barrier to the insatiable appetite for cloud – we continue to witness its meteoric growth. This has not gone unnoticed by the IT department nor the Board and they want oversight as IT is a strategic resource. There is the hint as to why we wrote this book – to meet the challenge of aligning an organisation's resources to grasp new opportunities of the digital age.

As cloud went mainstream a host of questions were initially raised.

- Can we really trust the safety of our data to the cloud?
- Will we get locked into a vendor with no get-out route?
- What IT stays on-premises and what goes in the cloud?
- Are the economics of the cloud superior?
- Will the cloud take away my job?

Depending on your point of view these questions have been resolved, and in any event, we have moved on.

The new questions are about how to harness cloud and plug it in to the prevailing BOM and ITOM and equip teams with access to the latest innovation. That has much more profound implications.

Disruption ahead? [1]

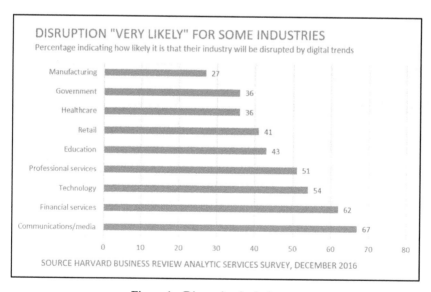

Figure 1 – Disruption by industry

---

[1] https://enterprise.microsoft.com/en-ca/articles/industries/microsoft-services/disrupt-yourself-or-risk-being-disrupted-competing-in-2020/

Cloud technology enabled a wave of disruption and some sectors of the economy have had their business model ripped to shreds. It all appeared to happen in a blink of the eye.

Right now, business leaders are wondering what the future is for their own business models as evidenced by this Microsoft report.

Some sectors (such as Retail) are probably forecasting less disruption because they think it has already substantially occurred. Maybe they are right, maybe wrong? Others such as Financial Services (especially Banking and Insurance) appear to be bracing themselves for disruption.

Disruption is distasteful and foretells change, and we all know that change is hard. Take careful note that some businesses recognised they should change but were too slow to react, and ultimately had to shut up shop. The agility of a business to anticipate and quickly react is critical and this is explored further in the next chapter.

It is a digital conversation

A new conversation has emerged, and it goes something like this:

> **Q.** Do we have a digital strategy?
>
> **A.** Do we need one?
>
> **Q.** What do you mean by digital?
>
> **A.** Well, it is something I am reading a lot about and it could be important to our future.
>
> **Q.** What is it?

There is no recognised definition for a digital strategy; it is whatever is right and appropriate for your business. It is widely understood that a digital strategy is not an IT strategy. Caution: Do not be led by the nose by new technology developments - although technology components will most likely be major elements in the delivery of the benefits of your digital strategy.

The configuration of the digital strategy brings together the business and IT teams' differing ideologies:

Business teams seek *agility* to respond quickly to the external environment, and IT teams seek *control* to manage the complexity of IT. Both need to evolve in a new harmony.

The new reality

The IT team are coming to terms with the fact that the 'good, but not great' IT Operating Model (ITOM) established to *control* their carefully managed 'Buy or Build' IT platforms for years is just too slow. It might be suited to core functions that are internal to the business such as HR and Accounting, but the external facing business teams need *agility* for their new 'digital at the core' Business Operating Model (BOM) to be competitive. The business is demanding speed of change, and the IT team is on notice to work with them to deliver.

In a moment of time the penny drops, and the linking of the fate of business and IT teams is realised: we need to communicate better, and change and do new stuff together faster, we need a new 'OM'; one that links our ITOM to our BOM more tightly and allows it to cycle faster, and we need it now!

The key to it all seems to be the cloud and these things they call DevOps and Agile ...

They shout in unison; **We need a Cloud Operating Model!**

So now read on to learn more about why a COM is at the core of every successful 21st century business.

Chapter 2

The Digital Wave

The world as we have created it is a process of our thinking. It cannot be changed without changing our thinking.

Albert Einstein (*Theoretical Physicist, 1879-1955*)

USINESSES generally succeed because they continually evolve (not always at great speed) and increasingly that is enabled by technology and interpreted as innovation. That innovation occurs in a couple of ways:

1. Take an existing business model and execute it in a better way than competitors. Deliver incremental improvements ideally at low risk and at low cost. Experiment and accept fail or succeed outcomes.
2. Devise an entirely different approach to meeting customers' needs and 'disrupt' the status quo. Figure how to serve the under-served customer segment(s) with a complementary economic model.

A business that delivers broadly the same as others, in the same way, might differentiate on service quality via improved speed or accuracy of delivery, or on less tangible metrics such as 'easy to do business with' or a strong brand image, and often even by just doing the same at a lower price. For established businesses a step-change in the business model is typically harder than bargained for. The process of delivering improvements is easier and where that relies on associated IT upgrade(s) then it often happens rather too slowly. That is the soft underbelly that the disrupter attacks.

The D word

A lot of talk about disruption is resulting from new business models using technology to completely change how a product or service is served up to the consumer.

Three very well-known examples are Uber, Netflix and Airbnb. These three companies entirely changed the way they their respective products were taken to market. The end consumer products were largely the same, it was the buy and delivery model that changed. They attacked (deliberate and intended) established taxi, video rental and (previously already disrupted) accommodation booking markets.

Whereas it was once the case that online was for the brave because of the security fears, today you can miss out completely if you are not online. You must also be exceptional, because other choices are just a click away.

As Microsoft report in its 'Disrupt yourself or risk being disrupted: Competing in 2020'[2] this is today's agenda.

Will you be disrupted?

Business leaders know their industries are ripe for transformation and are eager to bring the benefits of technology to their business. In fact, in a new study by **Harvard Business Review "Competing in 2020: Winners and Losers in the Digital Economy"**[3], 80% of the 783 respondents believe their industry will be disrupted by digital trends. Most of those (84%) said their industry has either passed the inflection point of disruption or will pass it by 2020.

Digital **leaders** are doing today the things they need to do to be successful in 2020. Companies that form their strategies now, shift resources to new digital initiatives, and redesign their organization and culture will have a distinct advantage. Micro revolutions occur typically every 12-18 months, so companies must be in a **continual state of transformation**.

---

[2] *https://enterprise.microsoft.com/en-ca/articles/industries/microsoft-services/disrupt-yourself-or-risk-being-disrupted-competing-in-2020/*

[3] *https://hbr.org/sponsored/2017/04/competing-in-2020-winners-and-losers-in-the-digital-economy*

History is littered with the graves of businesses which, when encountering a significant trend made the choice to do-nothing, took the wait and see option, considered they were too big to fail or did not react fast enough. It is wise not be complacent.

> In 1965, the average tenure of companies on the S&P 500 was 33 years. By 1990, it was 20 years. It is forecast to shrink to 14 years by 2026.

It is equally unwise to trivialise the decision, or to simplistically assume or be bossed into blindly accepting that all businesses must disrupt themselves. Let's review some very useful myth-busting content along these lines from the MIT Sloan Management Review[4] (Feb 06, 2017).

Myth #1: Every company should digitally transform.

Reality: Not every company, process, or business model requires digital transformation.

Myth #2: Digital transformation leverages emerging or disruptive technologies.

Reality: Most short-term transformational impact comes from "conventional" operational and strategic technology — not from emerging or so-called "disruptive" technology.

Myth #3: Profitable companies are the most likely to launch successful digital transformation projects.

Reality: If things are going well — defined crassly as employee and shareholder wealth creation — then the chances of transforming anything meaningful are quite low.

Myth #4: We need to disrupt our industry before someone else does.

Reality: Disruptive transformation seldom begins with market leaders whose business models have defined their industry categories for years.

Myth #5: Executives are hungry for digital transformation.

Reality: The number of executives who really want to transform their companies is relatively small, especially in public companies.

---

[4] Attribution: Stephen J. Andriole is the Thomas G. Labrecque Professor of Business Technology at Villanova University in Villanova, Pennsylvania

It is for you to decide if you recognise these myths characterise your organisation's stance. In the cold light of day, as some businesses operate in a market highly susceptible to change, then Myth #4 might be highly relevant. Transformation is easier in unregulated markets, whereas regulated markets are cushioned by the need for consultation and legislation that can slow down or inhibit radical change. In that case you have more time to anticipate and consider your move.

Intuitively, the answer for most must surely be to keep a sharp eye on the competition and hedge your bets.

The search for value

So, the things that qualify as 'transformation creating value' in businesses are often in the areas of cost efficiency and automation, or in being able to offer the customer a more bespoke product or service. There are other ways that value can be created in this traditional scenario – but all essentially fall into an efficiency bucket – doing the same things faster, cheaper or better than before.

The thing that is different about value creation in a disrupter model is that it: achieves a similar or better outcome to an existing business model in an entirely different way, or it delivers an outcome not previously available. Such disruption is typically a step-change.

Uber created an app to hail a taxi and know the approximate cost of your journey before you travel with a pickup time.

Netflix delivered new release videos on demand to your TV.

Airbnb allowed a homeowner to rent accommodation direct to the consumer. Some homeowners gave up their jobs to make a living out of renting a room. Wow!

Now successful businesses they have put others out of business or made it harder for them to compete. Thought provoking stuff!

Very few businesses truly 'disrupt' the status quo – and they are usually new entries. Even fewer established businesses take the risk of disrupting their status quo and cannibalising their core business, although of late this is something they're more pressured to do. And sometimes what is labelled as disruptive is just fixing something that was badly broken anyway.

Talking business models

The business model is the new challenger ground and the disrupter has a blank piece of paper and that puts them at an advantage over an established business that has many things to consider before they disturb their business model.

The accessibility of high-speed scalable cloud compute and clever 'off the shelf' code building blocks on a pay as you go basis is probably the single factor that has removed a great many of the barriers to entry that previously protected the incumbent.

Over the past decade technology has been the primary enabler for delivery of efficiency gains and for some doing things differently broadly under the heading of innovation. That same technology is also the engine for those hot heads with a great idea working in a garage or shared workspace and unencumbered by organisational politics and the rest that slow you down.

It is probably fair to say that, in the case of most new entry disrupters, their new business models have been entirely enabled by technology. Their definition of success is different, starting out from zero with very low costs they set out to win or steal revenue and do it as fast as possible. They innovate fast to stay ahead of those that are better funded and often end up being acquired by one of the incumbents they set out to disrupt.

Don't despair; there are ways for established businesses also to be a challenger and that is what Geoffrey Moore in his book Escape Velocity[5] calls the 'asymmetric bet'.

Now new entry disrupters don't need to read a book about building a Cloud Operating Model - they are 'born in the cloud[6]' and they know no other way. This book is primarily focused on the Cloud Operating Model (the 'COM') for the enterprise customer who has complexity by reason of their size, existing business model and IT legacy has most to gain, and most to lose.

Now – and this is an important observation – many of the business value improvements to date in the enterprise have not been

---

[5] Geoffrey Moore is perhaps best known for his work 'Crossing the Chasm'. Escape Velocity is relevant reading in support of this book's themes.
[6] Born in the Cloud – a business that from its inception relies entirely on the cloud for delivery of its products and/or services and customer services.

initiated by people whose core competency is technology. These businesses have not historically been 'wired' in a way that allows this to happen.

Instead these changes are often inspired by a visionary business leader who drives the technologists and the other people in the business toward an outcome which they instinctively believe is achievable. They set the challenge and provide the framework to facilitate the required change. This is often done by a mandate to copy or match a disruptor's new offering. Other times, by making a bet. The technologists in the enterprise are then invited to respond to the challenge of delivering on what and how.

Supercharge your BOM!

The Business Operating Model (BOM) is sometimes documented and other times just familiar and describes how an organisation delivers and captures value and sustains itself in the process – it is called work. The IT Operating Model (ITOM) supports the organisation's BOM and aims to meet its needs responsively and cost effectively. With the cloud you can now supercharge your BOM and deliver a new level of *agility* with a COM as we describe in this book.

In the enterprise IT world, we have become very accustomed to this demand/supply model for innovation – the business demands, and the technologists figure out how to supply.

When it comes to being truly innovative, this traditional operating model of Business - IT engagement has some major failings. In a world that recognises the probability of disruption is BAU then the role of IT in this mode of engagement with the business has to change.

The IT team has to be entrepreneurial and innovative, it has to take on a more detailed understanding of what differentiates the business it is a part of, and it needs to start making suggestions about how to be more competitive other than 'let's save some money by doing this better'.

Conversely, the business must adjust to be receptive to new ideas and some may be uncomfortable to live with, e.g. Artificial Intelligence. With innovation there is risk as well as upside.

It is the case those enterprises that have moved into the world of the public cloud now have new tools to apply to work. For example, the work of processing data to reveal new insights for the business to act on is accessible and affordable in the cloud to allow random experimentation and that was not possible ten or even five years ago.

Put simply, it's perfectly plausible that business executives 'don't know what they don't know' about their business and the market in which it operates. This is not a criticism just an observation and a trawl of LinkedIn reveals the insights of others on this point.

"

- *"The truth is, if you aren't using data appropriately your competitors probably are. "*

- *"Without big data analytics, companies are blind and deaf, wandering out into the web like deer on a highway"* **Geoffrey Moore author and consultant.**

- *"It is important for marketing professionals to improve their skills in data analysis. It takes time and skill to determine which pieces of data are meaningful. But this process of boiling down data into consumable chunks is imperative for getting buy-in across an organisation."*

- *"I hear this guy was pretty smart. At least that's the word on the streets. But seriously, without the data to support a decision, too much is being left to opinion and chance. Why risk it? Test and Retest."*

- *"One of the toughest things to do with analytics is creating a narrative that is easy to understand for colleagues and executives. Obviously, we know that visuals are important, but it takes more than that to get the type of buy-in you want. When deciding which pieces of data are the most meaningful, start from the end and work backwards. What am I trying to achieve? What does the audience need to know?"*

- *"The amount of information available is overwhelming. So much so, that managers and executives don't have the time or ability to focus on specific data sets."*

"

The cloud is awash with innovation and resources for a 'propeller head' (yes the business team still think they are even though they are highly skilled and highly paid and high in demand) down in the basement to cobble together all of the data that the organisation has held for all time, throw it at a 'pay by the second' public cloud data analytics module, and discover something completely new about the business that the leadership simply did not know.

For example; 'Did you know that our most profitable customers are not the ones we think, they are actually those that are ...! Or; 'Our fasting growing client demographic is actually ... - perhaps we should focus our marketing on that small but growing niche market?'

It is also now possible with the concepts of Agile software development and advanced coding tools, to test ideas quickly and at low cost and accept a fail outcome (nothing of interest there) is also a learning outcome. It is the new way and may feel uncomfortable at first. The IT team should be saying; 'Hey, we could knock that up on our website by Wednesday if you want to, put it out there to see what happens?'

So, the lessons to learn from the business viewpoint are that:

- You DON'T have to be a boffin or understand the digital jargon in order to be able to demand and achieve the delivery of value to your business in a digital age.
- You DON'T need deep pockets, simply access the economics of the cloud.
- You DO have to create an environment whereby the seeds of such change are nurtured and encouraged.
- You DO need to set the conditions for your IT professionals to develop an entrepreneurial mindset.

In a digital age, technologists within an enterprise are key players and must be fertile in thinking of ways to support the business to work smart.

> Work smart in a digital age takes on a new meaning; blending a culture that promotes ideation with use of technology to test new ideas.

Why should so many of the highly disruptive ideas come from start-ups? There is no reason and the response of many established businesses is to create an environment for new ideas in Innovation Labs and that is the way to go provided it is run with the discipline of a start-up! What does that mean? In the cloud! Work Lean,

Work Agile, accepting failure (no blame) and learning. Praise and reward the breakthrough.

People in the mix

The skill set of a business that puts its IT in the cloud has the opportunity to radically change as large swathes of operating IT can be removed. That can mean fewer people are required and/or people with different skills are sought after. Then there is the need to consider what key roles are needed in-house to drive the COM forward.

This can present a dilemma as to who can step up, or do you go outside to find those skills? While you can switch on technology really quickly the people in the mix require more time to come to terms with change. It can be tempting to outsource for expediency while the reality is you should keep a core 'tech' competency in-house, as this is a long game.

The Way Ahead

There are no constraints on the human mind, no walls around the human spirit, no barriers to our progress except those we ourselves erect

Ronald Reagan (United States President, 1911 – 2004)

I F only you could press the pause button as you ponder the seemingly endless assault of articles foretelling that your business model is going to be disrupted and what is your digital transformation plan and are you on top of your customer experience and the robots are coming. Oh, and then there is the 4th Industrial Revolution (4IR) characterised by a fusion of technologies that is blurring the lines between physical, digital, and biological spheres (isn't Wikipedia wonderful). There is a lot happening with much scratching of heads in terms of what this all means.

We are in a time of boundless innovation and it can send the head spinning with questions about its relevance. Is it a fad, will it pass? Many believed the cloud was a fad, something that would peter out and how wrong they were!

Even so we are left with choices; do nothing is always an option and otherwise make a bet, preferably a calculated bet. Every industry has a predisposition to adopt technology, for example:

- The retail industry has bet on eCommerce and if you are a retailer today and not online then the future is bleak
- The automotive industry has automated its supply chain processes and made extensive use of robots

The technology drivers of the 4th Industrial Revolution allow great scope for creative thought in terms of how they are applied to work and the replacement of human work by a machine. The role of Artificial Intelligence with its human description – The Brains – is an example of technology providing both opportunity and dilemma. This has caught the attention of politicians because of its societal impact and you can read Microsoft's evidence to the UK's House of Lords Select Committee on Artificial Intelligence[7].

The leadership team face challenging times balancing the desire, or perhaps necessity, to put technology to use together with its social responsibility. If you think that seems odd, then consider the difficulties that Google[8] and Facebook[9] have faced from regulators and politicians. With technology so deeply ingrained in society it has come under intense scrutiny with a new order of social responsibility for the leadership team to consider.

Do not fret. This book is mindful of all these influences yet practical in terms of its questions because the future is dependent on the decisions you make today.

4th Industrial Revolution

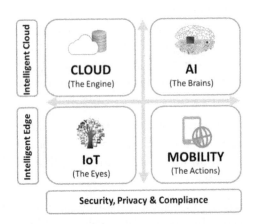

Figure 2 – The 4th industrial revolution

---

[7] *http://data.parliament.uk/writtenevidence/committeeevidence.svc/evidencedocument/artificial-intelligence-committee/artificial-intelligence/written/69654.html*
[8] *http://europa.eu/rapid/press-release_IP-17-1784_en.htm*
[9] *https://www.euractiv.com/section/data-protection/news/top-eu-privacy-watchdog-calls-facebook-data-allegations-the-scandal-of-the-century/*

Professor Klaus Schwab, founder and executive chairman of the World Economic Forum, describes how this fourth revolution is fundamentally different from the previous three, which were characterised mainly by advances in technology. These technologies have great potential to continue to connect billions of more people to the web, drastically improve the efficiency of business and organisations and help regenerate the natural environment through better asset management.[10]

You may have been an early adopter of cloud or just getting started, the evidence is that cloud is having a transformational impact on businesses and that looks set to be the future direction of travel, so a Cloud Operating Model needs to be the centrepiece of this conversation.

Watch this space

The new buzzwords Digital Transformation and Business Transformation are both popular and topical to how businesses are reinventing how they organise their work. The new way favours building teams that are agile and have a fail fast mentality while keeping overheads low. The cloud is highly suited to support this way of working and applicable to the micro business or goliath.

What is digital transformation? [11]

Digital transformation is about reimagining how you bring together people, data and processes to create value for your customers and maintain a competitive advantage in a digital-first world.

The COM is the vision of a business to deliver its 'value' by increasing its reliance on cloud computing (for some that may result in a cloud first strategy) to do that. The COM acknowledges the legacy IT (sunk cost) that will continue to support many vital functions and is often the system of record holding vital data about, finance, HR and customers to name a few. The driver for any discussion about technology is how it supports the business strategy. That drives the discussion about how to support the

---

[10] *https://www.weforum.org/about/the-fourth-industrial-revolution-by-klaus-schwab*
[11] *https://enterprise.microsoft.com/en-gb/digital-transformation/*

strategy with IT; do you upgrade the investment in legacy IT and extend its life or the cloud?

In a world where product development times are shrinking, product life cycles follow suit and the tempo of examining the various elements of the business model (the authors are fans of Business Model Generation[12]) in response to competitive forces[13] predispose the business operating model to cloud computing.

The conversation is alive:

There is much talk about digital transformation and why, who, what and how. [14]

Executive Mandate	Line-of-business led	Built on third platform
• Digital transformation is at the forefront of customer conversations and is a board-level initiative. Executives view the path to capturing this opportunity as becoming technology-centric to deliver new customer experiences.	• Line-of-business (LOB) leaders such as marketing, operations, sales, HR and finance leaders are being called upon to drive business model changes and technology decisions, and to facilitate digital innovation toward a technology-centric business.	• The new generation of technologies - big data, analytics, social and mobile - are necessary to enable the achievement of a company's digital goals. These technologies along with accelerators like the Internet of Things (IoT) and artificial intelligence (AI), will dominate the unprecedented increase in future technology spending.

From another point of view the Global Centre for Digital Business Transformation report:

The Global Center for Digital Business Transformation says[15] that "organizational change is the foundation of digital business transformation". That's because changing the nature of an organization means changing the way people work, challenging their mindsets and the daily work processes and strategies that they rely upon. While these present the most difficult problems, they also yield the most worthwhile rewards, allowing a business to become more efficient, data-driven and nimble, taking advantage of more business opportunities.

---

[12] Business Model Generation at *https://strategyzer.com/books/business-model-generation*

[13] Porter's five forces analysis at *https://en.wikipedia.org/wiki/Porter%27s_five_forces_analysis*

[14] *https://enterprise.microsoft.com*

[15] *https://www.imd.org*

In this book we discuss putting organisational change in place.

A search of 'digital transformation' on Google will deliver over 10M results so let's not dwell on who has the better definition. The job is to get on with it!

Whether you are struggling with or like the idea that cloud computing is going to be the principal actor in support of the business operating model then this book is written for you. This book is not a text book for 'transformation' of a business, rather it deals with the reality of a mega trend with the shift to cloud computing and access to the raft of innovation in the cloud. That introduces the role of a cloud service provider(s). The long-established IT Operating Model meets the new Cloud Operating Model that both shape the Business Operating Model.

Reality check

When did you last create a new product or service and <u>not</u> consider what IT was required to support that? It does not happen that way anymore and with cloud computing laying down a challenge to the past order of 'own and operate' there is both opportunity and complexity. This book in its two volumes exposes both.

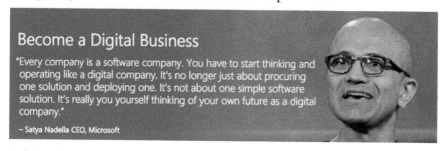

Become a Digital Business

"Every company is a software company. You have to start thinking and operating like a digital company. It's no longer just about procuring one solution and deploying one. It's not about one simple software solution. It's really you yourself thinking of your own future as a digital company."

– Satya Nadella CEO, Microsoft

It is hard to imagine an organisation without IT but what about describing your organisation as a software company and as a digital business.

- How do you feel about that?
- Is it alien or hard to accept as a reality?
- If digital were core to your organisation's existence what would need to change?

Unless you are a new business with no IT assets then the reality is what you have already invested in IT will survive until it no longer serves its purpose. What that means is that some existing IT will be 'lift and shift' into the cloud if that is the right thing to do and sometimes there is no reason for change.

What is changing is how we have moved away from thinking about data processing (hardware focused) and business processing (software focused) to how to quickly respond to the changing needs of the organisation and called out as *Agility*. Then the conversation is about how quickly the needs of the organisation can be satisfied and that is framed in the Cloud Operating Model.

Chapter

4

The Race is on

By 2020 every business will become digital predator or digital prey – which will your company evolve into?

Forrester Research

I

T is accepted as truth that today technology supremacy is used to create competitive differentiation. While it is acknowledged that is not easy to achieve, cloud computing makes technology highly accessible and affordable compared to the capital-intensive upfront cost and time to build and operate IT, and that is a mega trend[16].

Previously if your organisation wanted access to innovative technology it had to write a big cheque and choice may have been limited. The cloud is a magnet for innovation and presents a showcase of technologies that is suited to organisations of all sizes and low risk with free trials and instantaneously accessible on-off compute and storage available.

It is the tool fuelling a race that excludes no one and is reciprocally driving the growth of cloud and creating new companies and some very rich high-profile entrepreneurs - you will know who they are. For some this mega trend is a highly destructive force leading to the demise of organisations – you will also know who they are.

---

[16] Mega trends are global, sustained and macro-economic forces of development that impact business, economy, society, cultures and personal lives thereby defining our future world and its increasing pace of change.

You are a software business

Recently the penny has dropped regarding just how important internal software development (including Data and Business Analytics, Robotic Process Automation etc.) will be to the differentiation of businesses in the future.

The COO's business mantra with regard to software development for the past 10 years may well have been distilled down to: 'I will avoid software development like the plague', or 'Software development is like standing under a cold shower and tearing up £10 notes'. 'We are a Bank, not an IT company'.

This mantra reflects the position of those focused-on cost saving. Only the wasteful will seek to develop software that is readily accessible in the cloud (and probably better than that developed in-house) available on a Software as a Service (SaaS)/Pay as You Go (PAYG) basis to do the 'must do' things in business such as running Email and HR, which every business has to do.

Yet this 'let someone else' do it approach misses one major point.

How do you truly differentiate against your competitors? How do you innovate?

Can you truly rely on third party software developers to deliver the custom very specific and complex features that you seek to be different, and to do that in a timeframe that suits your priorities?

And if they do, who owns the IP? If it is the third party then those same features will also soon be available to others, including your competitors!

Put another way, if every business took the approach only to use software from third parties, then don't they and their competitors all end up being more or less equal?

So, in reaching an agreement that innovation and agility are essential for differentiation, and that almost all innovation will come from technology (and software development specifically) isn't it now essential for a business to conduct at least a small amount of software development? Even if it is just to analyse what the data is telling you about your customers' buying patterns, and how you then analyse that to better understand how to serve your customers better and/or faster?

Buy, Build, or Both?

Historically, inherited CIO/COO wisdom has been that there are two real choices for acquiring software. 'Buy' Commercial Off The Shelf (COTS) packages or 'Build' your own bespoke solution.

We have long developed in-house enhancements to 3rd party software, so the 'Buy and then Customise' option is really an extension of the 'Buy' solution.

The Pros and Cons of these alternatives including on-going software lifecycle costs are well debated, so we won't dwell here. Now there is a new option. The combination of no or low commitment Pay As You Go software licencing models (SaaS), and recent (little known) availability of massive amounts of 'above the IaaS line' functionality within the public cloud platforms enables what is probably best called a 'Rent the Building Blocks' model.

If your thinking is to deploy public cloud as a way of decommissioning your datacentre then don't overlook the opportunity to decommission legacy software and change the focus of future development functions. The idea here is that today and in the future, in-house 'coding' is most likely to manifest as the gluing together of these off the shelf 'Building Blocks'.

This is the orchestration of cloud services with the implementation of a cloud operating model. To what purpose?

The ask of your IT team is; you want to analyse a dataset and need that fast. The IT team take the dataset, clean it up inside Azure Data Factory, put it into an Azure Data Lake, build a cube to present it and visualise it using Azure Analysis Services and display that in Power BI. Four different services, working in harmony, with nearly zero code, completely customisable and tuneable. Some of the language here is tech speak yet the point is that the IT team now have available the tools to rapidly respond to your ask.

You no longer need coding gurus (except possibly for maintenance of legacy systems) as Microsoft has done the heavy lifting. This is creating new roles for architects who keep control of the plan for the house that you are building, and 'business savvy' bricklayers who know how to glue the pieces together to extract value from your data.

So here we have described how the boundaries between IT and the business are broken down so you can react fast (agility) and we leave the translation of that for your organisation to you.

What is on the shelf?

Answer: Just about everything you can think of, and a whole lot more you didn't know existed.

The author's definitions are below, although there are slightly more detailed (and technical) explanations here: *https://nvlpubs.nist.gov/*

Software as a Service (SaaS)

SaaS applications revolve around the user. They are shrink-wrapped applications, delivered remotely, priced on a per user, per-month basis. They typically provider extensive customisation and configuration to align them to the demands of your organisation.

They are though, by definition, pre-packaged and not everything in the way they operate can be customised. They do, however, have fixed, predictable costs and very little (if any) maintenance requirement. Think of Office 365. You bring the users, Microsoft does the rest.

Infrastructure as a Service (IaaS)

IaaS revolves around the server. IaaS has a lot of similarities to a traditional on premises, virtualised environment. You can run your servers, much the same way as you do today, inside a provider's datacentre. The major difference from what you have today is the level of automation and scripting you have available to you. You also have, for all intents and purposes, unlimited capacity to create and delete virtual servers on the fly. You have complete control of the operating system, storage, networking and more. Think Azure Infrastructure Services. You bring the OS, Microsoft manages the hardware and virtualisation tiers.

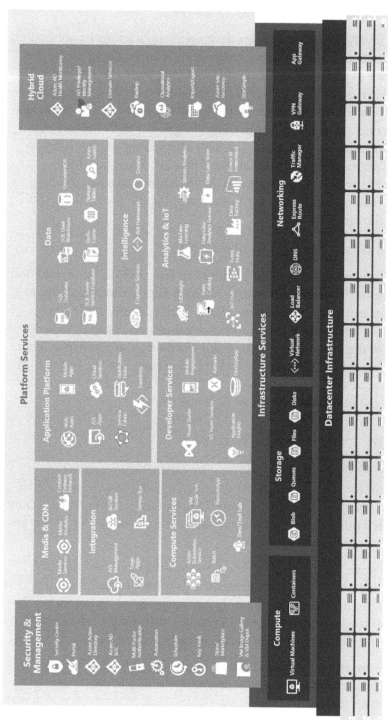

Figure 3 – Azure Service Map

Platform as a Service (PaaS)

PaaS revolves around custom-developed applications or application components. You can build an application by stitching together a number of platform services and deploying code on top of them. You have complete control at the application level, i.e. what the app is and how it functions, but you have less control of the actual mechanics of how that application is deployed and managed, the cloud vendor does that for you. This also means you have less to maintain, support or worry about. Think of Azure platform services such as SQL Azure and Azure Kubernetes Service. You write the code and deploy it as a managed application, Microsoft does the rest.

Functions as a Service (FaaS)

FaaS is an evolution of PaaS, with even less control, but in addition even lesser management responsibilities. It provides the ability to execute raw code, as a service. With PaaS, you still need to be aware of and pay for a web server, for instance, even if you don't have to deploy or manage it. With Functions, you just deploy your code block and Microsoft will charge you based on the number of times your code actually executes. Think of Azure Functions. You bring the raw code, Microsoft does the rest.

What does this deliver?

Whilst FaaS is still relatively new, the other three services are extensively used today. In some cases, organisations have gone all-in and completely removed their on premises equipment, replacing it with a mix of these three capabilities. Those old server rooms are now meeting rooms!

They serve the purpose of delivering 'on-demand' functionality. For example, enabling infrastructure to grow on demand and shrink on demand with you only paying for what you need. Previously those costs would have been absorbed as a fixed cost to meet the highest forecast volume of transactions.

These are the capabilities that when exploited can cost effectively create real competitive differentiation, and they are the starting position for the disrupter.

We're now moving the discussion firmly into the future world of "application engineering in the cloud using microservices" – so we will press the pause button on the tech until volume 2.

Who controls the cost?

There is a widely recognised and obvious potential downside of allowing techies to have unlimited on-demand PAYG computing resource. In fact, for many business people the fear of an unexpected enormous invoice for services used is probably right up there in their top 3 cloud fear list.

So, the emergence and adoption of public cloud governance systems is now on the rise. Organisations want to be able to budget for a certain amount of project compute time, bill the time transparently to the incurring division, pre-emptively sign-off on limits and breaches – just like all of the traditional things that finance, IT and the business have done (or wanted to) for years.

Organisations that do opt for multi cloud (note the warning in next volume on that), need tools to help them determine pre-emptively the "Best Execution Venue" for their production cloud workloads – from both a performance and cost viewpoint. These technologies are still maturing, so the required governance workflows can be difficult, although not impossible, to achieve.

Later we'll also touch on the harder to solve topic of cost and quality governance in an Agile development world.

The business head conversation

The business conversation about adopting Agile and using PAYG public cloud services needs to have a different focus. This conversation has to centre on the view that the services described above are the enablers for new ways to get ahead.

It is not fanciful to keep an eye on mega trends as they shape the world and the price of ignoring them can result in extinction. Think about the retail businesses that ignored the trend to online retailing and even the technology companies that thought the cloud was fanciful and described it as nothing more than a return to the days of the mainframe – how wrong they were.

The business head conversation should not be wrapped up in technology, rather it should focus on staying relevant and competitive. In his book 'Hit Refresh', Satya Nadella CEO of Microsoft calls that out as four initiatives[17]

1. Leverage data to improve the customer experience
2. Support employee productivity with mobile collaboration tools
3. Optimise, simplify and automate business processes
4. Transform products, services and business models

Turning those initiatives into practical solutions is the next step and will increasingly bring into focus some specific mega trends that are shaping and, in some cases, worrying society[18]:

Artificial Intelligence (AI)

It is early days for AI and there are lots of examples that you may have already been exposed to. For example; have you visited a website to see a pop up with a Chatbot? That is a practical, yet simple use of AI at work.

Big Data (BD)

It is often not the case that we have too little data, rather too much to make sense of and provide the insights we seek. Somewhere buried in the data are nuggets of insight if only they could be exposed. You could put hundreds of people to work on what is frankly a thankless task, or you can use a computer and run 'n' scenarios in parallel in a matter of minutes. That is Big Data at work.

Robotics Process Automation (RPA)

Factories around the world are advanced in their use of RPA. Now RPA is coming to the office and automating routine and repetitive Human/Computer interaction tasks. Insurance firms are beginning to "staff" the email response agents in their call centres with "robots" who can read, process and respond to common email queries without human involvement. That is RPA at work.

---

[17] From Hit Refresh ISBN 978-0-00-824765-2 Page 126.
[18] The US Government set out its position in a paper (May 2018) at
https://www.whitehouse.gov/briefings-statements/artificial-intelligence-american-people/

Now you may or may not be ready to put these capabilities to work. However, one thing is a given and that is the cloud is an enabler, and so building a core competency in cloud is fundamental to being ready to use these capabilities as they become relevant to your organisation.

Don't get caught out

The amount of data being created daily is truly astonishing and so too is the computing required to store it, index it and make it available to search. Now part of the pursuit of an improved business is to find better ways to process and analyse data. In short order – to use it intelligently. There is no shortage of ideas how that can be done, and it is a big task and one that has more than just technical challenges. The new challenge is *coming to terms with what you are allowed to do with that data.*

As you investigate the possibilities to put the technologies referred to above to use, it is vital to understand the regulatory framework governing the use of data defined as personal identifiable information (PII). In Europe the General Data Protection Regulation (GDPR) came into force on 25th May 2018 and substantially upgraded the rights of EU citizens (about 512M as of January 2018) to control how their PII is used and curbed the freedoms of businesses to do as they like when processing PII. So, on the one hand technology is becoming ever more capable of processing data and extracting the insights you seek. On the other hand, your hands are tied how you use the data. This is not prohibitive; it is not a case of big data 'or' data protection. It is recommended to read the guidance[19] published by the UK's Information Commissioners Office (ICO) related to AI, BD and RPA. That guidance topped the votes in the People's Choice Award at the 39th International Conference of Data Protection and Privacy Commissioners (ICDPPC) in Hong Kong (September 2017).

> So, tread carefully with the adoption of technology for the processing of PII and always check what compliance must be observed and keep in mind that compliance is not globally harmonised.

---

[19] *https://ico.org.uk/media/for-organisations/documents/2013559/big-data-ai-ml-and-data-protection.pdf*

Undercurrents

Technology is so ingrained and important to society that it is on the agenda of governments.

This is a recent phenomenon, with a growing interest by policy makers in regulating the technology sector while not stifling innovation. Should this put a stop on your plans? No. The very institutions that policy makers work for, or are elected to, have similar challenges to businesses but on a much greater scale. They need technology to advance their work. Even so it is wise to recognise that the techno-political debate is hotting up, and if you work in the media industry you will know that only too well. Keep a watching brief and talk to Microsoft who, because of their size and influence are party to the techno-political debate.

Do you treat IT as a key tool in the race to get ahead? We hope this chapter has at least convinced you to begin to do so. The extent to which software development will differentiate your organisation from competitors will vary wildly across industries and where you add value in the chain. If you are in one of the industries most likely to be disrupted, and you haven't invested in Agile yet – then you had better read on. The gun to start the race has already been fired!

Chapter

5

Agile – small word quick work

Perfection is not attainable, but if we chase perfection we can catch excellence.

Vince Lombardi (American Football Player, 1913 – 1970)

DEPENDING who you ask what agile is, they will tell you it is about moving quickly, or, they'll probably tell you that Agile (with a capital A) is to do with software development and that it's particularly helpful for software development projects where innovation with an uncertain outcome is expected. Both are correct. Here we refer to Agile. For the leadership team the thing to know is that if you want to be agile then Agile makes that happen.

The key difference between Agile and the standard coding methodologies for projects that preceded it is that Agile has as concepts:

- short term bursts (sprints) of coding
- regular face to face meetings (daily stand-ups)
- small teams that have a range of specialisations
- test, fail quickly, avoid wasted effort and speedily change direction
- coordination of small coding activities in parallel (rather than big ones in a serial sequence – hence the dominant predecessor's name "Waterfall").

Agile has for the most part become the de facto mechanism for software development in recent years. You can do Agile coding without DevOps and/or cloud. You can use DevOps and/or cloud without Agile. They just happen to have evolved in broadly similar timeframes and they co-exist in an organisation or a project very well.

It is not our goal to explain Agile development to you. What's interesting about Agile within the context of this leadership volume is to explore its impact on the organisation as a part of the ITOM/BOM/COM discussion and to position how Agile is about so much more than just software development. Agile and its bigger brother, Scaled Agile Framework® (SAFe®) for Lean Enterprises, are the glue that blends these three operating models together.

Why did Agile evolve into what it is today in the application development space?

Agile aligns today's software developers with the needs of the business that is continuously in search of innovation. It is fast. Much faster than methods used previously, and it is that speed that supports the business to respond to change. Whether that change is planned, or in response to external events.

We live today in a business world of 'accelerating change at an accelerating rate'. In this new world, horizon scanning and taking a long-term view of what innovation will keep the business competitive, is simply not viable. The ability to react to the availability of new innovation and do so quickly is *as important* to being competitive as *the innovation itself*. Read that again as it is fundamental to Agile's raison d'être.

Innovation in the cloud is continuous and available to all-comers. In times gone by, those with the resources (deep pockets, skills) would outgun others. That is no longer the case. The competitive landscape has been levelled and actually tipped in favour of those that do not have the burden of legacy systems to maintain. Do you see the problem for some?

The central tenant of Agile is the backlog. Think of it as a long wish list. Every couple of weeks you pick new things from your wish list and deliver them. Because you only ever pick things off your wish list every couple of weeks, you can change tack much more quickly to respond to changes in priorities and external factors. The backlog is the central reason why Agile is so … agile.

Agile budgeting and forecasting

One of the biggest challenges with Agile is how you go about implementing it. Delivering small, discrete projects with Agile is relatively straightforward as it doesn't profoundly impact how you budget for these initiatives or require you to make wholesale changes to your processes. To truly embrace Agile, you need to make a few more major changes to the way you think about projects, budgets and deliverables.

Traditionally, both the business and IT tend to think about IT projects through the lens of applications and projects. We need a new application, or we need to change an existing application, let's create a project and align resourcing and budgeting around this project. This is the wrong approach.

Instead, organisations that a truly embracing an Agile approach are doing things a bit differently. Instead of applications and projects, start to think about the notion of a product. This may be an internal or external product. Drop the functional specifications and handoffs between business and IT.

Instead, assemble a cross-functional team, comprising business experts, developers and other members of the organisation in one cohesive, stable unit. Cross the business and IT chasm.

A large medical-device manufacturer significantly shortened its time to market by refining its organizational structure. Under its traditional structure, there could be as many as 20 handoffs when a business unit shared its specifications and requirements with the technology organisation for a new piece of software or an additional feature in existing software. Because of the interdependencies among its products, leadership knew it wouldn't be enough to deploy agile within one business unit or within certain product-management teams in the technology organization. In 2015, the company tweaked its product-ownership model so that software requirements were directly transmitted from dedicated product owners in the business units to the agile teams, rather than passing through multiple parties. With the change, the company was able to reduce the amount of time it took to release products in the market. The structural changes also facilitated the rise of several communities of practice. These role-based or topic-based groups (sometimes called guilds) are critical in agile-at-scale environments.[20]

Getting the team structure right and changing the culture is but one aspect of the transformation you must go through. One of the

---

[20] *https://www.mckinsey.com/business-functions/digital-mckinsey/our-insights/an-operating-model-for-company-wide-agile-development*

most difficult changes to navigate is that of budgeting and financial planning. Historically, IT budgets were set every year and there were often painful trade-offs between different projects and initiatives the businesses were driving IT to deliver. Instead, align these budgets to these product domains and empower product owners to direct this funding throughout the budgeting cycle having regards to changing business priorities.

The Disciplined Agile Consortium[21] has lots of great content to help with formalising this budgeting process:

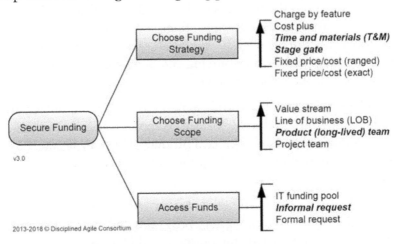

Figure 4 – Agile funding models

An interesting concept which is becoming more prevalent is the concept of venture-funding product development internally. In the same way a team of entrepreneurs might approach external parties to fund new products and services, now internal teams can vie for funding from internal investors. Initial funding might cover an MVP and then, directly linked to the success of the product with employees or customers, additional funding can be made available. This interesting approach laser-focusses budget in line with success and therefore significantly reduces wasted expenditure and cuts development running out of control.

Whatever approach you take to Agile budgeting and planning, ensure you major on flexibility and adaptability, whilst maintaining close visibility and overall control of your all-up spend.

---

[21] *http://www.disciplinedagiledelivery.com/secure-funding/*

Taking Agile Further

Agile is about so much more than just software development though. Agile has started to permeate just about every part of the business and has become a useful tool to manage almost any project you might want to run. What's interesting is how Agile can become the mechanism you use to run your most important project of all – your digital business operating model. This is where SAFe® comes in.

So, what is SAFe®? Several years ago, Dean Leffingwell wrote a book called Agile Software Requirements[22]. It became a best-seller that gave the world its first glimpse of what would eventually be known as SAFe®. It described a framework—called the "Agile Enterprise Big Picture"—that visualised how to apply Lean and Agile practices and principles to the Team, Program, and Portfolio Levels.

The concepts behind the Big Picture drew from the knowledge pools of Lean, Kanban, Scrum, and Extreme Programming (XP), as well as Don Reinertsen's The Principles of Product Development Flow. The distillation of these concepts into a single framework was applied in places like IBM, Discount Tire, John Deere, and Nokia with inspiring results.

Today, SAFe® is in its fourth iteration and has been adopted by 70 percent of the Fortune 100.

In its most simplistic form, SAFe® provides a framework for managing multiple business-focussed streams of work within an enterprise. A kind of backlog of backlogs. It defines these within the context of portfolios of epics, or major initiatives. An epic might be a new product that you want to launch. It might be a major technology refresh programme you want to undertake. It might be a new market you want to enter. It can be anything.

SAFe® provides a mechanism to manage and then prioritise these major initiatives and provide a bridge into both the IT and business teams that might enable this epic to be delivered.

Underneath the portfolio (epic) level is the program level. Epics are just that, epic! Each epic is broken down into a series of features

---

[22] *https://www.amazon.com/Agile-Software-Requirements-Enterprise-Development/dp/0321635841*

and enablers which are grouped into a program increment, which is a time-bounded period where you deliver some form of business value. This value is managed by an agile release train. Within each program increment, you have a number of scrum teams who actually deliver the work. Over, you'll see a diagram showing the high-level view of this process.

The thing that is most interesting about SAFe® is its applicability across such a broad range of initiatives you might be running as an organisation. The fact that by using SAFe®, Agile can be applied to far more than just software development. Agile budgeting and planning can now be used to represent and manage the entire innovation pipeline within your organisation.

As an IT organisation, your responsibility becomes standing up, feeding and watering a given number of downstream agile sprint teams. These multi-disciplinary teams will span different technologies. They will have different skillsets. They will do different things. But they will be there, willing and able, to work through the constant stream of requirements delivered up and prioritised by the business. No more functional requirements. No more detailed business cases. No more friction between the business and IT. Peace, and hopefully, harmony.

This brief description doesn't begin to do justice to the intricacies, or power, of SAFe®. When you fully understand it and see it in action, you will appreciate its power and how useful it can be. For more information on SAFe®, please see *www.scaledagile.com*.

What we seek to do here is simply to signpost you towards SAFe and to start to think about how Agile, applied at scale, can be that bridge between the business and IT. A bridge between your BOM and your ITOM.

Here is the authors' forecast: The businesses that crack the implementation of Agile development and the power of public cloud will be the businesses most likely to succeed in the next decade.

So, the most important objective for the implementation of a Cloud Operating Model is to create the way for real time interactive collaboration of the business team with the technology team. It's called Agile. It's that simple. Next in Volume 2, we get to the job of making it happen!

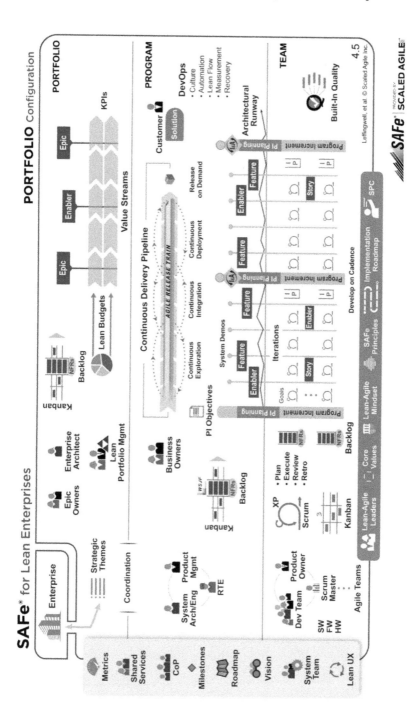

Figure 5 – SAFe® Portfolio Configuration © scaledagileframework.com

Agile – small word quick work

Chapter

The Business Questions

You can focus on things that are barriers or you can focus on scaling the wall or redefining the problem.

Tim Cook (Apple CEO, 1960–)

IN recent times the leadership team have been subject to increasing scrutiny of their understanding and oversight of the technology that is a foundation of the business. That does not mean to say they have to explain how the organisation has embraced DevOps. It does mean they need to be ready to talk about and explain the commitment to build an organisational capability to put technology to work in this digital age – and the core of that conversation is explained in Volume 1.

We have divided these questions into the same structure as the chapters within the first volume above. If you need some context around the questions, flick back to the chapter to which they refer to give yourself a quick reminder on the rationale of the question, or to help you best answer it.

There are no right or wrong answers. As this book suggests consult others and seek advice your vendors or from a business partner. This is important work.

1. **Section A** – The Digital Wave
2. **Section B** – The Way Ahead
3. **Section C** – The Race is On
4. **Section D** – Agile - small word, quick work

6.1 The Digital Wave

Have you encountered and organisation that only deals with others by phone and post? No, we are in a digital age and it is expected of every organisation that they understand what that means. We talk about that as a digital wave and it is unstoppable. The words disruption and transformation are so topical now so what is your conversation?

In this chapter above, we discussed the environment that is driving the agenda of organisations as they consider:

- Business model and its relevance in a digital age
- Disruption – what disruption?
- Creating Value – the output of transformation
- The Business Operating Model (BOM)
- The extraction of value from data

We will now give you some questions to ask about these topics.

☒	Question	Why this matters
☐	6.1.1 Has your industry experienced disruption from new entry technology-based alternatives?	If you are operating in a sector that is already used to disruptive change (like Retail or Media) then you are already attuned to understanding the impact of change. If your sector has long-standing tradition and/or is regulated (like Finance, Accounting and Legal) then there are good reasons why it hasn't had a major impact so far. That does not mean to say major changes are not coming. For example, the consensus view is that Retail Banking will soon be disrupted, and that developments such as blockchain, process automation, machine learning and artificial intelligence will soon turn professional services sectors on their heads.
☐	6.1.2 Is the board on-board with cloud?	The availability of on-demand pay as you go computing services means that the business team's ideas can be quickly tested, and quickly deployed into production. The application of Agile, cloud and DevOps are fast becoming established structural pillars in organisations that are innovative with their use of technology. The speed with which your organisation can reactively and/or proactively test and deploy new ideas is now a critical attribute for many organisations.

☒	Question	Why this matters
☐	6.1.3 How do you characterise the current state of adoption of cloud by your competitors? For that matter how do you think they characterise you?	Before you start to worry if your competitors are about to steal your lunch, ask what you know about your and their state of readiness with cloud computing and the associated advanced implementation toolsets? Microsoft[23] suggest three states of readiness: Foundational: Organisations with little to no cloud experience are still envisioning cloud and require end-to-end guidance for cloud adoption. Intermediate: Organisations with foundational cloud experience. Have an understanding of cloud technologies and are either evaluating or have migrated non-priority workloads to the cloud. Advanced: Organisations with advanced cloud experience are in the process of cloud adoption and want to optimise workloads on the cloud. When did you last check the available sources of information that show the uptake of cloud computing in your sector? Are you a leader or follower? Should you be investing in being a leader?

[23] Extract from Adopting the Microsoft Cloud Operating Model

☒	Question	Why this matters
☐	6.1.4 How dependent is the delivery of your Business Model on IT?	Take a guess. Ask others and compare. What does that tell you? The business model has many moving parts and a supply chain and value chain. It relies heavily on fast and efficient collaboration and that comes with complexity. If your business process is heavily dependent on IT for ordering, inventory management, delivery and the like, then you are more likely to be able to benefit from (or suffer from) IT (cloud) related disruption. Are you actively exploring how your customers want to be served and delivering the optimum customer experience, because if you are not then you may lose out to others that are attentive to the search for smarter (to include cheaper) ways to do that.
☐	6.1.5 When did you last review how the partnership works between the business and the IT team or your IT partners?	If your organisational structure does not support a bidirectional exchange of ideas with the IT team, then you might be missing out on a raft of innovation opportunities. Many of the new functions offered by public cloud computing platforms are complex and understanding the potential they have within your organisation can only be done as an open collaborative on-going discussion. We have an idea and want to? Why? It makes it easier for us to serve our customers. What do you want to change from how you serve them today? If the answer is technology, then the IT team/partner needs to be right in the mix of what is available.

☒	Question	Why this matters
☐	6.1.6 When did you last review your competitive position?	IT is the enabler and deliverer of an increasingly digital world and cloud computing which makes digital more accessible to organisations of all sizes. What that means is your competitors who may not have the resources you have, because they do not have the capital, can now use cloud to compete on a level playing field. That is a game changer. Are you in this new game? Are you seeing more new entrants in your sector? Are they having an impact?
☐	6.1.7 Do you see (and treat) IT as both a threat and a potential competitive advantage?	IT now needs to be tightly linked to everything from strategy to delivery, and Board level representation is now mandatory. If your organisation still treats IT as a supply and demand relationship, then you may be missing out on the know-how of your IT team. It is most likely that disruption will come at you from a technology-based platform – are you protecting that flank?
☐	6.1.8 Have you considered how you might optimise your customers' 'shop' and 'convenience' experiences using technology?	If you take heed of where much of the major disruption in many sectors has occurred, it is in these two areas. Specifically, how clients search and shop for a product or service, and then how conveniently (and sometimes how quickly) that is delivered. Many urban dwellers value convenience and time more highly than a price differential – so they will gladly pay more for these improvements.

☒	Question	Why this matters
☐	6.1.9 Do you have a culture to encourage innovation?	If you believe innovative ideas can come from anyone then the culture needs to be able to elevate those ideas to the appropriate discussion forums. Some believe innovation should be centred within a Lab format with a budget and start-up culture. You need to enable and actively promote the propagation of ideas, trial and error, and reward the effort (rather than the result) no matter which model you adopt. Don't expect overnight results – this process takes time particularly in large organisations. The result may in the end be the one great idea that saves or supercharges the organisation.
☐	6.1.10 Do you collect data, or do you distil it into much its more valuable cousin, information?	Organisations collect an ever-expanding universe of data – with an associated cost to retain and protect. The real value of data is revealed by the science of Data Analytics (aka Business Intelligence). Data is data and what organisations strive for is value from that data and extraction of that value is a function of people and technology. Do you have those resources? .
☐	6.1.11 Does your technology team understand what your business does, and what makes it different to its competitors?	If not, then you have some training and investment work to do. You can't expect the IT team to contribute to the innovation agenda if they don't 'get' the basics of the why, what and how of the organisation's existence. The history of IT has pigeon holed technologists (they just do tech). Not anymore, they are key to unlocking the potential of technology for transformation of the 'always done it this way' and delivering 'new ways' to innovate (overused word but forget it at your peril).

☒	Question	Why this matters
☐	6.1.12 Are you set up to think and act like a challenger or more steady as she goes?	Taking a bet to disrupt a business model (to be a challenger) is a major decision point for most organisations, but if you don't prepare for it, history informs someone else will. If you want to be a challenger what do your answers to the questions before say about your readiness?
☐	6.1.13 Which of the myths exposed in Chapter 2 did you most readily agree with?	What does that tell you about your organisation's current stance? Have you discussed this with others in the organisation and is there a consensus? If there is then you may be susceptible to 'group think' so, consider inviting independent external validation of your stance.
☐	6.1.14 How would you characterise your capability to process data into information?	This is one test of your organisation's agility, the capability to react to an event with the analysis of data to reveal insights to support decision-making.
☐	6.1.15 When did you last perform a skills audit of your IT team?	The capability of your IT team to support the organisation's digital journey is make or break. What skills gaps does this book expose?
☐	6.1.16 Do you have a committed budget for the CPD of your IT team?	Big changes are occurring with the availability of cloud services and your team need to be ready and equipped to face off the challengers to your business model as many of them are born in the cloud and cloud savvy.
☐	6.1.17 Is your IT team competent to present the organisation's value proposition?	In the past it may not have mattered yet today with IT at the core of the organisation's value proposition it is vital. Those that set out with disruptive ideas understand how technology underpins the value proposition and that is becoming a key attribute of an organisation equipping itself in this digital age.

☒	Question	Why this matters
☐	6.1.18 Do you have an Innovation Lab?	You may ask; why do we need one? If you accept that your current business model may be under threat of disruption, then where is the source of new ideas that will the spark of your reinvention?
☐	6.1.19 What skills are needed for your core 'tech' competency?	6.1.15 would reveal your current skills. Are they skewed to support existing IT assets? What are the skills you consider to be core 'tech' competencies for the next five years? This book will help you answer this question.
☐	6.1.20 What is the organisation's appetite to use cloud services?	The own and operate model for IT is a comfortable place albeit with an overhead. There is a gravitation to the cloud (evidence its meteoric growth) and that can challenge that comfortable place; are you being left behind? If the future is a growing reliance on cloud services what are the implications for you?

6.2 The Way Ahead

What is the capacity of your organisation to absorb change?

What is driving that change?

It seems that technology is at the core of change and the rate of innovation is hard to keep up with. Still you don't want to get left behind so you need a plan and that is bigger than the selection of technology.

In this chapter above, we discussed the drivers of change and some of the big implications that weigh on the leadership team as they consider their responsibility to stakeholders.

Some questions follow to spark the conversation to shape the way ahead.

☒	Question	Why this matters
☐	6.2.1 How does your organisation think and talk about digital transformation?	Is this a live conversation or background noise? Who is taking the lead; the business team, IT team, or have you as this book promotes joined up? For some digital transformation has become a catch all (a budget winner) for all of the pre-existing change that was already occurring. Others have decided on implementing one initiative, e.g. let's create a mobile App for our clients. In reality, a digital transformation programme should be on-going, focussed on reinventing parts of the business model, incremental and agile (vs. monolithic and large scale).
☐	6.2.2 Does the IT function have a seat at the top table?	If most organisations are becoming (in part at least) highly specialised 'digital' organisations, then surely it makes sense to have digital represented at board level. Go one better and appoint NEDs with digital experience to challenge the status quo.
☐	6.2.3 Are you looking for clues in your data to inform the business about what actions to take?	A digital business uses its data as an asset, sweats it to reveal hidden nuggets of information. It is a new science and not that easy to do. A machine can process data much faster than humans and analyse it according to rules. Yet it still needs to be eyeballed by someone who can interpret the data generated by machine processes. Machine and human combined. It is fast becoming mainstream for an organisation to develop this machine and human competency. Are you?

☒	Question	Why this matters
☐	6.2.4 Do you access the experience of your staff?	Technology is pervasive in our lives and for some it is a hobby or even an obsession. Younger generations change their preferred mode of communication with increasing frequency, and they seem to intuitively know which application to use (this week) for which purpose. They pass this knowledge (with much rolling of eyes) to their older friends and relatives. This latent skill set in your employee base is valuable to the organisation. Do you provide a way for your people to share ideas with an incentive to do so? And do you listen when they do? Perhaps the new young hire in dispatch has some great ideas – will they remain just ideas or maybe deliver a quantum improvement in the work of the dispatch team?
☐	6.2.5 Go big or small?	The word transformation conjures up big change but that is not the only way. One approach is to begin a process of micro-segmentation of smaller parts of the Line of Business application suite, reimagining and making them cloud native as you go. Another is to look outside the organisation and to learn what others are doing and consider if that is an option. To quote Deloitte[24] from their report Courage under fire: Embracing disruption; 'digital should be defined based on business needs'.

---

[24] https://www2.deloitte.com/global/en/pages/risk/articles/directors-alert-courage-under-fire.html

☒	Question	Why this matters
☐	6.2.6 Is IT viewed a Cost Centre or a Profit Centre?	If the IT function reports into the CFO or the COO, then a cost centred IT mindset is most likely. Splitting off a chunk of IT and aligning it with the line of business management functions will likely yield results that would not otherwise be available. The business needs to be able to engage directly with IT implementation functions and the IT functions need to be able to understand and feedback directly to the business leads. Breaking individuals out of the IT function and spreading them throughout those teams, and perhaps even the more radical approach of devolving some IT functions completely to the business and deploying a well-coordinated matrix management approach will deliver on *Agility*.
☐	6.2.7 Is change feared?	Who likes change? We've been here before when cloud was the hot topic of conversation for the IT team and thoughts turned to; so, what does this mean for my future? Putting the IT team alongside the business team breaks down this fear as the IT team is integral to the success of the business team. No conflict of interest arises and what needs to get done, gets done.

☒	Question	Why this matters
☐	6.2.8 How do you set the stage for the future you are envisioning?	'I hate unsolicited spam emails!' is a common complaint from workers at all levels, and sure, some are just downright inappropriate and unwelcome. However, this never-ending stream of approaches and offers is still one of the best methods of easy to access competitive intelligence, new ideas and market data. Attitude to spam and making time to attend educational events is an interesting cultural litmus test. Most employees are simply too busy to conduct untargeted, open-ended outbound market research. Should you provide filtered commuting time reading from sources that are curated under the direction of the leadership team?
☐	6.2.9 Is digital on the agenda of every board meeting.	The financial crisis of 2007-8 revealed no organisation is too big to fail. More recently the failure of organisations is often linked to the fact their business model did not evolve with changes in the external environment in which they operated. In an increasingly technology driven world the board is dealing with a new phenomenon; taking ownership of the digital strategy for this is becoming a new benchmark of the board's competency. Too busy - then consider creating a committee tasked to advise the board on all matters related to the use of digital.
☐	6.2.10 Who owns the COM?	There is no right answer to this question. The COM upon its implementation becomes an organisational practice – the way we do things around here. Look at other practices embedded in the organisation and what works best. Read 6.2.4 again.

☒	Question	Why this matters
☐	6.2.11 What capacity and competencies do you think you need to develop software?	In this book we advocate keeping a core 'tech' team that is interfaced to the business teams and has competency to translate the needs of the business and deliver a solution whether that is developed in-house or available in the cloud. How many and what competencies do you need to retain?
☐	6.2.12 Who has the responsibility to stay abreast of what public cloud services can do to enhance your competitive edge?	This is creating the art of the possible and fits with the experimentation that is so easy to enable in the cloud. Ideas can flow from the business teams to IT or vice-versa and someone has to be a translator and up to-date with what is available from public cloud services. Public Cloud vendors are releasing new 'above the IaaS line' functionality almost every day. These features and functions might just present exactly the functionality you are looking for, so you don't have to build it – keeping abreast of these developments is important to driving tech-led innovation.
☐	6.2.13 As the balance of expenditure on cloud services versus legacy systems changes what is the impact on the business case?	There is always competition for expenditure and a hurdle rate for deciding which projects get the go ahead. With legacy systems you had to justify capital expenditure and the recurring cost of support/maintenance over the lifetime of the project. With public cloud it is on/off and you only pay for what you use. As a quip: If its not paying off, then just turn it off!

☒	Question	Why this matters
☐	6.2.14 Have you evaluated if a 'cloud first' strategy right for you?	Cloud First is interpreted, as the solution to a requirement must first be met by cloud and only if that is not viable then consider an alternative. This principle is applied and tested against what is most important to the organisation, for example: Scalability, Resilience, Agility, Cost, Innovation and Compliance to name a few. Cloud is not the right answer for some workloads. Large enterprises support an IT legacy and the decision as to whether or not you should 'lift and shift' this legacy into the cloud is complex and certainly non-trivial.
☐	6.2.15 Do you have (or are you) an internal cloud evangelist (supported by a senior cloud champion)?	It is not always the case that everyone will be on-side of the cloud and so having an evangelist ensures that there is a balance of protagonist and antagonist. In the culture of most large enterprises where change can be glacial by nature, find an energised evangelist give them the support they need and let them do their thing.
☐	6.2.16 Have you identified your 'Lighthouse Project?	The term lighthouse project refers to a model project that aims, besides its original purpose, to have a signal effect for numerous follow-up projects as they look towards it for inspiration and guidance. Therefore, in addition to success, a great notoriety is intended (Thanks Wikipedia).

☒	Question	Why this matters
☐	6.2.17 Do you understand the concept of 'above the IaaS line' benefits of Public cloud?	Many today still completely miss the real value of public cloud. When NIST[25] first defined cloud in 2012 many disagreed with some elements of the definition because they weren't at that time widely available! The legacy of the confusion (and the adjusted temporary working definition used for much of the ensuing period) means that today, many still see cloud and IaaS as synonyms. They are not. The real value of public cloud in the future will come from the exploitation of the PAYG[26] availability of Platforms and Functions as a Service (see Chapter 4).
☐	6.2.18 Are you in a position to exploit these 'above the IaaS line' benefits?	The cloud may deliver bottom line savings and the point here is to ask if you are just switching on cloud or also mobilising people to work differently. To truly be cloud ready your organisation needs to move away from concepts such as servers and monolithic application suites. The very essence of the server based model for how we deployed applications in the past creates implicit scaling restrictions. Ideas such as microservices, and the micro-segmentation of applications are shaping the future of both in-house and third party cloud native application development. If you have not expanded the edges of your IT environment into the public cloud, then accessing, integrating and using these tools to exploit your data and work differently just isn't viable.

---

[25] National Institute of Science and Technology
[26] Pay As You Go

☒	Question	Why this matters
☐	6.2.19 Have you begun to explore mechanisms for enabling (whilst still governing) the use of Public Cloud?	The potential for runaway cost explosion is one objection inhibiting adoption of cloud. An important aspect of your production cloud environment is ensuring that cost transparency and management reporting is inbuilt. To satisfy this demand there has been an explosion in the availability of tools – use them.
☐	6.2.20 Do you engage independent market analysts?	If you only listen to vendors, you get a vendor specific view and while there may be legacy compatibility issues and loyalty of a long-standing relationship to consider the choices available in the cloud are vast and independent market analysts can offer new perspectives. If you take a moment to think about the diversity between early adopters and technology laggards in the cloud world it is more pronounced than in any preceding iteration of IT change. The cloud savvy have accelerated away from the pack. Accordingly, trying to catch up with the leaders using only your own resources is unlikely to work. Skilled resources in this space are very sought after – so get some help.
☐	6.2.21 Do you have your own #challengers platform?	The #challenger is your internal secret weapon. Young, analytical, 'tapped in', socially active and aspirational. By providing a platform for your #challengers to bring forward ideas, and significantly rewarding them for doing so by sharing the rewards is one way to keep a #challenger mentality alive and attract more to your firm.

6.3 The Race is on

Ten years ago, few would have described technology as a race and it was only necessary to watch what your peers were doing and tune in to what your preferred vendors were saying. Today that has that all changed with the economics of the cloud and a dazzling array of innovation being churned out fast and all accessible not only to your peers but also those plotting to disrupt your business.

If that feels uncomfortable – good, because if it did not then you would be complacent and that is not where you want to be.

In the past a CEO would not usually be asked a question about technology. If they duck the question today alarm bells start ringing. If you read the news, then you will know the CEO carries the can for technology – success and failure. Clearly, they are not expected to deliver a sermon on Agile (Chapter 5) rather they are expected to articulate the big picture of how the organisation will respond to the opportunities of this new era of technology on tap.

Some questions follow use them to go layers deeper in getting to a known position that everyone on the leadership team is comfortable with.

☒	Question	Why this matters
☐	6.3.1 Do you wait for innovation to come knocking on your door?	Some organisations appoint a person or small team to go hunting for and be the receptor (to suppliers) for absorbing innovation. A detailed understanding of the business is needed to recognise opportunities to put new ways of working to use enabled by technological innovation. If digital is at the heart of every business, then you will want that to be the very best it can be. Do you expect innovation to find you, or you to find it?
☐	6.3.2 Are you measuring the right things, or are you just focussed on measuring things right?	Sometimes we can't see the wood for the trees and we follow the old patterns because that's what we do. Data is the new science and art of business in the digital age and a major focus for the industry that develops software to analyse data and customers with data to analyse. Don't recognise this? Perhaps you do not have the expertise in-house - so then look outside for assistance.
☐	6.3.3 Are you in the race?	It may or may not matter? Every organisation will have some interest in how they stack up against others. Are you investing in technology or investing in building a capability to use technology? They are not the same. Few organisations would say they do not have enough technology, rather it is the case it is a heavy load to carry. The COM described in this book is about building a capability to support the 'business, people and technology[27]' for this digital age.

---

[27] As reported in Microsoft's document 'Adopting the Microsoft Cloud Operating Model'

☒	Question	Why this matters
☐	6.3.4 When was the last time the board was presented an opportunity and risk assessment of all data held by the organisation?	Data is a strategic resource and the board is accountable for the organisation's strategy. It is also accountable for oversight of risk. The board's task is growing in complexity as it weighs opportunity and risk associated with data. How do we take advantage of AI while complying with our legal obligation to data privacy? The new smarts are building an organisational culture that sees customers' data as an asset for building trust and not blindly applying technology to analyse the data. Do that well and it is a win-win.
☐	6.3.5 Are your people still tied to the office?	Productivity is easy to define, often hard to measure and an endless pursuit. The race for a work/life balance, reducing the waste (and environmental impact) and cost of commuting time and convenience of mobile working is wrapped up in the productivity sum. The cloud has been an enabler of mobile working. Have you explored all the opportunities available in the cloud in your pursuit of productivity?
☐	6.3.6 Are your business processes customer and employee friendly?	In an age where convenience is highly valued and aided by technology then throw in some friendly. Making friendly can be as straightforward as making something simple and reducing the work. None of us is as smart as all of us[28]. If you are looking for innovation to apply to your processes then the cloud is the place to look, that is where smart people (developers) make available innovation.

---

[28] Quote attributed to Kenneth H. Blanchard

☒	Question	Why this matters
☐	6.3.7 Do you say: so what to transformation?	If it ain't broke, don't fix it. True enough yet in a fast-paced world the new skill is anticipating what's coming down the road that will knock you down. It is then a question of how quickly you can react to new situations be they threat or opportunity. In this book we promote the cloud as the foundation for delivering *Agility* and building a competent organisational practice around a Cloud Operating Model gives you that capability to respond quickly. The bedfellow of anticipation is preparedness. You are smart, you work out the rest.
☐	6.3.8 Have you done your homework?	Right now, there is frenzy of new technology matched by a frenzy of ideas as to how to put that to work. The oil in that engine is data, your data, and a lot of that data was obtained under consent. In some cases, you are a custodian (Data Controller and/or Data Processor) and not the owner of that data. Before you throw your data at new technology e.g. AI, check your legal obligations and talk to your Data Protection Officer. You are familiar with the responsibilities of a Data Controller and Data Processor? If not, you have homework.
☐	6.3.9 Have you evaluated the opportunity and threat of AI?	Whether you are a leader or follower it is valuable to have a position on technologies that have the potential to transform work. AI is in this category. How would you classify your current position? No position, under review, quantified, applied? AI has the potential to replace human work and that has many implications to include how it may impact your HR planning.

☒	Question	Why this matters
☐	6.3.10 Have you evaluated the opportunity of Big Data?	The recent European Union General Data Protection Regulation (GDPR) has put data, and particularly Personal Identifiable Information (PII), in sharp focus. Before you plough ahead with Big Data check those involved understand the seven principles[29] of GDPR and engage a Data Protection Officer in case of any doubt. If your tech team is not aware of these principles (and many will not be) then they could land the organisation under risk of investigation by the regulator with potential for significant financial and reputational harm.
☐	6.3.11 Do you have a position on the impact of Robotics and Process Automation (RPA) in your sector?	The promise of RPA is hotly contested with great differences of opinion about its impact and in particular the displacement of jobs. If you are an employer, then you have a social responsibility to take into consideration. Conversely, RPA could be used by competitors to undermine your business model and so it is wise to be alert to this threat. Are there jobs that you have difficulty filling or retaining staff? Is that a safe place to expose RPA? Have you considered the use of RPA to release dependency on off-shore processing?

---

[29] *https://ico.org.uk/for-organisations/guide-to-the-general-data-protection-regulation-gdpr/principles/*

☒	Question	Why this matters
☐	6.3.12 Do you have a vision for your business in a digital age?	If you look back 5 and 10 years what has been the impact of technology on the work of the organisation? Probably you will identify that technology has had a big impact and more recently the cloud will have driven that agenda? So, in your vision what are digital capabilities that your organisation must excel at and why are they mission critical[30]?

[30] A **mission critical** factor of a *system* is any factor (component, equipment, personnel, process, procedure, software, etc.) that is essential to business operation or to an organisation. Failure or disruption of **mission critical** factors will result in serious impact on *business operations* or upon an organisation, and even can cause social turmoil and catastrophes. Source: Wikipedia

6.4 Agile – small word big work

If you want to be that organisation that innovates and delivers a true digital experience for your customers and employees, you need to become more of a software company.

The key to combining your business operating model (BOM) and your IT operating model (ITOM) into a cloud operating model (COM) is to define a common interface and language between the two parts of the business along with a mechanism to work effectively together.

Agile is well established in the software engineering space, but increasingly is moving into every aspect of service creation across the business and IT.

Harnessing additional intellectual property on top of Agile in its raw form can serve to create additional value. These questions help you to address some of these issues.

☒	Question	Why this matters
☐	6.4.1 Do you employ software developers and data analysts?	You would be amazed how many organisations in this day and age for whom the answer to this question is "No". If you do employ software developers, then don't stop there. They should be focussed for at least some fixed percentage of their time on working with the business teams to identify vehicles for COMPETITIVE ADVANTAGE rather than being bogged down 100% on menial break fix tasks.
☐	6.4.2 Have you invested in Agile training – and not just in the IT team?	If the business and IT are to begin to engage in iterative ongoing Agile development and innovation, then a good starting point is to make sure everyone understands the big picture and reasoning behind such an approach. Organisation wide training on the concepts involved is good use of budget at this time.
☐	6.4.3 Do you have an experimentation budget?	The IT and Business Team staff need to have some flexibility to try (and fail) at new ideas, and to do so they need a "slush fund" with which to experiment.
☐	6.4.4 Do you measure the average time it takes for your organisation to move from idea to delivery?	Such a measurement will often reveal a surprisingly slow (glacial even) innovation cycle. You may think you're reacting quickly, but if you take all of the steps in the process into account you may be surprised.

☒	Question	Why this matters
☐	6.4.5 Do you constantly test your marketplace?	Even if you think you have tuned your customer experience to be the best it can possibly be, you should never stop teasing and testing your marketplace. The adoption of radical idea that changes an entire sector can often be simply a factor of target market maturity or timing. You should begin to adjust your mindset to be as happy with a failed result as with a successful one. Failure can teach you a great deal more than success. What your clients DON'T want is very powerful information.
☐	6.4.6 Have you considered doing a "lighthouse" project	Rather than being top down mandated, Agile is often best embraced by an organisation as a part of a process of enthusiasm infection. Pick a high profile, low risk example project – such as maybe that time reporting system that everyone hates – and use a process of iterative feedback and improvement to make it sing. This will allow everyone to see and participate in a successful example of agile at work and let them understand how it can benefit their customers' experiences too. They will be lining up to drive their own project next.
☐	6.4.7 What is your mechanism to budget for and deliver new services?	When you're looking to do something new, such as launching a new service, as the business you will typically look to IT to envisage, quote and deliver a project. Individual projects and the budgeting associated with this can cause excessive delays and require detailed functional specifications which can change rapidly in this fast-paced digital world. You need to consider alternative mechanisms for interfacing with IT.

☒	Question	Why this matters
☐	6.4.8 Have you considered having an always-on innovation team?	One way to avoid excessive governance and overhead on innovation is to establish teams of digital specialists whose sole job is to work through a backlog of innovation imagined by the business. There is a fixed, budgeted cost for this team per month and its efficiency can be measured via the velocity of new capabilities they are delivering.
☐	6.4.9 How would we manage these teams?	One of the advantages of having projects and budgets is to help track the success of these projects. Success here is, however, often measured in the number of reports and artefacts created. Moving to a more Agile model of innovation management can have significant advantages, such as measuring progress in terms of value delivered to the business.
☐	6.4.10 How would we report on this innovation?	Agile in its raw form is good at getting things done, but poor on reporting what has been done. "We'll keep going and let you know when we're done" isn't very helpful. Frameworks such as SAFe® can provide the required structure, business alignment and reporting that traditional project management methodologies attempted but failed to deliver.

Building a Microsoft Cloud Operating Model

'What the technical team need to know'

Chapter

A new operating model

The definition of insanity is doing the same things over and over again expecting a different result.

Falsely attributed to Albert Einstein (Theoretical Physicist, 1879 – 1954)

Why do we need a new operating model?

IN recent years, IT has been viewed through a lens of cost reduction. A successful CIO or CTO was one who tamed the flow of cash exiting an IT department's shrinking budget and tried tirelessly to tune an already well-oiled machine to extract additional value and productivity out of it.

Processes were brought in for every aspect of IT operation to both streamline and to control.

Information Technology Infrastructure Library (ITIL) emerged as the dominant industry-accepted viewpoint of what an efficient IT operation looked like. ITIL included Service Design, Service Transition and Service Operation across a range of realms including Availability, Configuration, Testing, Release, Knowledge, Change, Event, Incident and many more. It became, and is still viewed now, as the epitome of what good looks like.

As we read in the first part of this book, with any business or IT operating model, there are two competing forces of agility and control at play, whatever the shape or size of the organisation. There is a business operating model which thirsts for agility and an IT operating model which strives to deliver control.

The historical trend of the last two decades towards outsourcing has served to further enforce this traditional divide. The business yearns for new capabilities, services and business models, whilst the incumbent IT partner looks to maximise profitability through resisting change and increasing control. The very concept of outsourcing rests on the premise that an outsourcer can typically deliver an IT service substantially more cost effectively than an internal team. Part of this can be delivered through specialisation and economies of scale, but it also naturally depends on a slick and highly controlled operating model which penalises (through change control) doing anything differently from the way it works today.

The very concept of change control is central to much of the business' frustration with a traditional IT operating model. From a business perspective, why are we being penalised for wanting to do something better and differently from the way we are doing it today? Especially if it increases customer satisfaction and/or delivers new services which we don't deliver today? Changing something means we have found a better way of doing it.

But the business doesn't get it right? Change is hard. Change is difficult. Change is risky. Change is dangerous. Change is something to shy away from and discourage.

Throughout this book we want to try and challenge some of these preconceptions and the subtext that exists at pretty much every organisation on the planet that change is but a necessary evil.

We want to try and imagine a new model together.

We want to try and construct a new relationship between business and IT. A new grand bargain. A new world where IT lives within the very kernel of an organisation's business operating model. Where IT sits at the top table from a strategy perspective and feels empowered and valued to drive real differentiation in the organisation's marketplace.

To do this, though, IT departments need to learn to behave differently. We need to be equal partners rather than just service providers. To understand the context of requests we are fielding and to become more proactive with recommendations, suggestions and new models. To become far more deeply engrained within the business operating model.

The business also must learn to behave differently. It needs to stop thinking of IT as a support function, detached from the important work of actually running the business. Something to put in a box and try to do as cheaply and efficiently as possible. A nuisance getting in the way of making more money. It needs to start thinking of IT as strategic advantage and digital differentiation within an increasingly cut-throat market.

When the entire organisation lines up behind giving customers and employees the best experience, the biggest difference is the attitude towards change. For both actors in the equation, change becomes something positive to embrace. Something to invest in. Something to covet. Not something to shy away from or discourage.

The changing roles of CIO, CTO and CDO

The Chief Information Officer (CIO) role has changed over the years as the organisational requirements changed when it came to managing computing systems and the data they stored. In particular, the CIO was the officer in the company responsible for all elements of the organisation's data and was the chief data custodian. This didn't last; as we moved closer to the Y2K years the role of the CIO moved more to one of financial control and long-term planning for IT systems within the organisation. In particular, the requirement to be able to best understand the computing needs of an organisation 3 years out, and CIOs being judged on how accurate they could be with so little data about how the changing conditions of the world would change the requirements of the organisation's required IT capability and spend.

Ever since the cloud PAYG (pay-as-you-go) model arose, so too has increased power been granted to the Chief Technology Officer (CTO). More importance was placed on the person responsible for making the correct choice in the short term as well as the long term. With less weight being placed on the cost of IT and more on how organisations could get a ROI from their IT spend, the CTO and the Chief Financial Officer (CFO) teamed up and we have observed the notable decline of the CIO role.

In the last 5 years, and with the recent cheap and effective adoption of machine learning and AI services being available to drive insight into an organisation's data, the requirements have changed again.

Now, with the world of data ever changing and the important and value data holds in organisation, the role of the CIO has emerged again... but interestingly enough, it's being reimagined as the CDO (Chief Data Officer) role in the organisation.

From an audience perspective, it's important to make the distinction as the CIO is definitely still looking at cloud from a dollars perspective including the operating model that comes with data and next generation workloads. The CTO cares about the adoption of innovation and ROI on technology adoption, which also means the operating model. In this new model, change can be made and a safe environment to fail is adopted both culturally and technically. Finally, the CDO role is important as we are seeing that as being the first C Level role that is truly driving the adoption of public and in some case multi cloud ... taking advantage of the power of AI from one cloud whilst leaving standard workload management to another.

How is a Cloud Operating Model different?

A Cloud Operating Model (**COM**) shares many similarities with a traditional IT operating model (**ITOM**). The fundamental difference revolves around how to deal with change. It describes a model where IT continues to deliver everything it has always done in terms of driving stability and availability but allowing this to persist in a world built on change. Built on a world where everything changes, all the time.

A traditional IT operating model starts from the pretence that change is difficult and dangerous. Things often break when you change them.

What if we could build a model where change is not dangerous, or at least in orders of magnitude less dangerous? That model is what we will try and construct, together.

Chapter

Strategy and service providers

Simplicity is the ultimate sophistication

Leonardo da Vinci (Polymath, 1452 – 1519)

Setting off in the right direction

THE first step on a journey to a Cloud Operating Model is to build a cloud strategy. A move to the cloud is a big deal. It's a big decision. A decision that will permeate every part of your business and impact on every aspect of your existing IT operations model. It can be risky. It's not something you do lightly.

Building this strategy can be involved. It's going to mean engaging a lot of people, across your business. You're going to need to get buy-in from everyone that this is something that we all want to do and if not fully, then to what extent.

You might canvass your business and try and build a case to move to the cloud and the consensus might just be either no, or lukewarm. They might say that it's just too difficult. Our IT is too elderly. We can't move our data to the cloud. We are so super special, and we just can't do it.

We understand it's hard. Cloud is not right for everyone. We wish you all the best. Maybe we'll speak again in the future.

Nearly all organisations start with this conception to some extent though, even ones that have now fully embraced cloud. To be successful you will need buy in from the business and from the key IT stakeholders. As Friedrich Nietzsche once said, *"He who has a*

why to live for can bear almost any how." So is true for businesses.
Without a "why" this can be a very difficult path to strike out on.

For everyone that's left, let's get down to business. We'll assume
you want to do this and so it's not if, it's how. We'll assume you
landed on something like "Cloud First". Cloud wherever possible,
unless there's a really good reason why not.

Example of Guiding Principles for IT Strategy:

1 All applications and workload services currently hosted should be assessed for cloud migration.

2 A single user identity must prevail over all service consumption.

3 IT service delivery must be adhere to a service-centric model which includes lifecycle and evergreening.

4 All new services should adhere to a technology code of practice and architecture, in particular:

    a). Based on open standards: services should interoperate with little or no remediation.

    b). Cloud security principles: services must meet the security requirements for handling data and privacy.

    c). Public Cloud First.

    d). Native functionality cloud services is preferred over 3rd party tools.

5 All new services should use public cloud services in the following priority order:

    a). SaaS.

    b). PaaS.

    c). IaaS.

6 All cloud services, including IaaS, will be owned by customer but can be managed by 3rd Party service providers.

7 Simplicity and reliability of use for end users is of the highest priority.

8 Access to services must be restricted to permitted users and devices only and based on least privilege.

9 End user devices must be control by security policies and guidelines geared for a Mobility First strategy

10 Native functionality in client devices and access services is preferred over 3rd party tools.

11 Automation and predictive insights, where possible, must underpin the support, remediation and administration
of the services delivered.

Figure 6 – Guiding principles for IT Strategy

Once you've got the green light, we'll need to drill in to the detail.
What does cloud-first mean? How do we build a strategy around
this? We first need to understand what cloud really means. This
book is not designed to educate the reader on the NIST definition
of cloud computing and get drawn into a debate about what is and
what isn't really cloud. We'll skip a step. When we talk about cloud
within the context of this book we are talking, predominantly
around public cloud. Hyperscale cloud. The providers that invented
the concept, not those who rebranded their existing offerings.

A true cloud strategy should also focus predominately on public
cloud if you really want to harness the innovation we spoke about
in the first volume. If you really want to digitally transform your
organisation.

We then need to break cloud down into the three main food groups, IaaS, PaaS and SaaS. Again, this book will not dwell on these definitions and assumes the reader has a level of understanding around these concepts at a high level. Your strategy needs to be cognisant of the differences between these service models and speak to each individually.

Communities of Practice

A great place to start on a journey to building these standards and service-centric patterns is to leverage communities of practice around each one of these service models.

Within a community of practice, teams come together to build the guiding principles on an ongoing basis but are only ever seconded and eventually look to dissolve themselves out of the centre again and back to the front line.

Vendors and partners can work together to assist in establishing these communities of practice. Internal anchor tenants are selected for the cloud and planning, and strategy is established through consultation with consultants and the team. The first few tenants are migrated, and the cloud practices are established. On completing the teams start to return to their original teams and enlist more people into the community, looking to have them work on patterns and practices that strengthen the overall cloud community.

Multi-Cloud

The two building block services for your core infrastructure will be IaaS and PaaS - server hosting and application hosting. According to Gartner[31], you now only have a small cohort of true cloud infrastructure providers to choose from, Amazon, Microsoft, Google, Alibaba, Oracle or IBM. Assuming you don't have significant operations in China and that you're not locked in to Oracle or IBM, that leaves three.

The decision you then need to make is "do I as a business support, one, two or all three of these providers?"

---

[31] *https://azure.microsoft.com/en-gb/resources/gartner-iaas-magic-quadrant/en-gb*

First of all, we need to clear up what all of this means. You have the concept of Multi cloud, the concept of Hybrid cloud and for some very large organisations you may have both.

Let us begin by exploring the concept of Multi-cloud and Hybrid cloud so we are working off a common understanding.

The concept of Multi-cloud is a highly debated topic right now with some in the industry defining the concept as a common technology layer hosted by multiple vendors while others define it more like a deployment model that requires a common abstraction layer between different environments.

For the purposes of this discussion we will treat the concept of Multi-cloud as one that requires the management of different cloud service providers, both public and private, with differing tools and services in a common way.

To extrapolate on this, if you were to, say, decide to provide a suite of IaaS services from more than one cloud provider, you will need to factor in the tooling and process you need to ensure that services deployed into one cloud met the same configuration and governance standards as another.

To achieve this, even for something relatively simple as a single virtual machine host, you may be required to replicate effort in the management and maintenance of service blueprints and the deployment of management tooling into multiple locations. Your brokering and orchestration layer, whether highly automated or invoked on demand by staff, would need to support multiple methods for addressing the cloud provider fabric which is largely bespoke for each vendor and the tools required for service management would also need to incorporate the subtleties of each vendor's cloud service environment.

There are of course ways to abstract this complexity by consuming lower level services such as containers, but most heritage IT estates are a long way from being able to move more than a small portion of services to using this type of technology.

There are a number of vendors and platforms which seek to provide this abstraction for you, but they can be complex and expensive. They also often fail to surface niche platform-specific capabilities from different vendors, such as Azure Cognitive Services.

There are some good reasons for going Multi cloud and there are also bad ones.

A good reason may be something like a scenario where you were consuming services that lent themselves to a specific public cloud provider while having other services that lent themselves to a different provider. If you find yourself in this situation you may be forced into a multi cloud world by your application layer.

In this model you may find yourself consuming SAP S4/HANA public cloud as well as Oracle, IBM Bluemix, AWS, GCP and Azure.

Alternatively, a poor reason for consciously choosing a multi cloud approach would be the fear of vendor lock in and the concept of being able to move workloads between vendors to get the best point in time price point.

We will argue in this book that the increased management complexity and operation risk of this approach far outweighs the perceived risk of committing to a given cloud provider. Also, many cloud providers charge you for offloading data from their services so an architecture that is moving vast amounts of data between cloud providers doesn't necessarily make sense.

Hybrid Cloud

Having set the scene for Multi cloud, lets address Hybrid cloud.

This concept is much easier as it relates to the location of services within a single management boundary.

Microsoft launched Windows Server 2012 R2 as the "Cloud OS" with the idea that if you were running Hyper V and System Center across your on premises estate, your service provider and were consuming Azure public cloud services, you were in effect within a single management plane and could shift workloads around to meet whatever business and technical drivers you were faced with.

This conversation has matured over the years with the introduction of technologies like Azure Stack which allows for a near seamless operating model across these three physical hosting options.

For those without the deep pockets required for Stack you can still get a high level of integration out of the box between your on premises environment, a third-party hosting provider and Azure.

So, Hybrid cloud can be seen as a location-based paradigm within a single set of management tools.

Microsoft adds weight to this by providing tools like Azure backup, Azure site recovery and the Operations Management Suite of products that will run across On Premises and Azure providing you a unified management plane for these operational services.

So now we have bedded down the concept of Multi and Hybrid cloud we will look more closely at some of the architectural concepts that will define the model you adopt.

Your estate

We like to look at IT estates at a high level as being broken down into Modern Data Centre, Modern Workplace and Modern Application.

Your strategy will be informed by the capability and direction of travel of the services across these three domains. Your strategy will in turn inform the business on the approach to each domain for your individual organisation based on what your business and technology drivers are.

Much of what we talk about spans all three of these domains.

How you reimagine your end user compute services to incorporate public cloud will have a direct impact on how you architect your modern datacentre and how you deploy applications to it.

Before we go too much further we have to discuss a key aspect of this new IT world you are imagining.

Bimodal IT

One of Gartner's more recent concepts is Bimodal IT[32]. This concept describes a model of operation which supports a blend of heritage IT assets alongside newer, more agile cloud-native capabilities and service lines.

---

[32] *https://www.gartner.com/it-glossary/bimodal/*

Bimodal IT = Marathon Runners + Sprinters

Think Marathon Runner	Mode 1		Mode 2	Think Sprinter
	Reliability	Goal	Agility	
	Price for performance	Value	Revenue, brand, customer experience	
	Waterfall, V-Model, high-ceremony IID	Approach	Agile, Kanban, low-ceremony IID	
	Plan-driven, approval-based	Governance	Empirical, continuous, process-based	
	Enterprise suppliers, long-term deals	Sourcing	Small, new vendors, short-term deals	
	Good at conventional process, projects	Talent	Good at new and uncertain projects	
	IT-centric, removed from customer	Culture	Business-centric, close to customer	
	Long (months)	Cycle times	Short (days, weeks)	

Gartner

Figure 7 – Bimodal IT © Gartner Inc

This Bimodal IT concept is a really important one to wrestle with and grasp the significance of. We will expand on this more throughout the book but the relevance for this in the scope of this strategy chapter is to understand the core differences between the modes and how the closer to Mode 2 you can get, the more valuable the IT organisation will be to the business.

The primary focus of the two modes is summed up in their respective goals.

The goal of Mode 1 is reliability which can be translated to up time or stability. This mode is geared to fight change and to focus effort on driving efficiency out of the IT estates under management.

Mode 2 however is all about change. Change is good, change brings new ideas to bear quickly and allows business agility.

As you prepare your IT strategy to incorporate public cloud services you need to think about how you architect services to best leverage the fast pace of change in public cloud.

There is an imperative to move your IT organisations further along the cloud maturity model to allow your services to respond to the fast pace change at the business level.

The nirvana here is to allow your businesses to realise revenue from an idea by enabling IT services quickly.

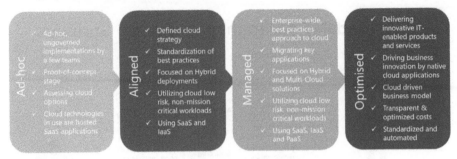

Figure 8 – Cloud Maturity Model

These IT services should be designed in such a way that they can be spun up and down on demand and the maintenance and health of these services should be highly automated.

You may not achieve all of this in the first pass, but the closer to the optimised model you get to more benefit you and your businesses will realise.

One of the keys to success here and the reason this concept is called Bi Modal IT in the first place is that you need to do both. You can't just abandon your Mode 1 heritage IT estate in pursuit of cloud. This estate is running your business today and much of it will be running your business 12 to 18 months from now.

It is also important that you begin to incorporate some notion of services architected for native public cloud.

Many organisations begin by introducing small applications and services that supplement existing, deeply embedded Commercial Off The Shelf (COTS) applications.

An example of this would be something like extracting key data from an on premises line of business application into an Azure Data Lake, then writing a mobile phone application that uses this data for a single business function in a read only mode.

A business process updates data in the application, the data lake gets updated and someone's mobile device goes "ping" informing them of a new event or piece of information relevant to their job in near real time.

A small eco system of applications and services like this can spring up around a core LOB application and add huge amounts of value without having to spend blood and treasure on trying to re-engineer the core application to fit natively in cloud.

At some point the major software vendors will rewrite their applications to be installed natively into public cloud but until then you will need to support your IT in both modes.

Service Provider Relationship

One of the most important parts of a move to a COM is a change in the relationship between you as a customer and your cloud vendor as a service provider.

Historically Microsoft, Oracle, IBM were companies you bought software from which you either ran yourselves or paid someone else to run for you. It supports a classic ITOM where responsibility for the software was separate to the responsibility of delivering it.

Whilst there are occasionally things which the software vendor does which cause you real pain, such as a bad update, the majority of the time you are responsible and in control of your IT destiny/service.

If something goes down, anyone up to the CEO can come down and get increasingly grumpy until you actually fix the problem. Whereas their presence typically doesn't add much value and in fact often has the opposite effect, at least they feel better that they are mucking in and helping to get the problem solved.

In a cloud world, typically, these functions are blurred. The creator of the software now delivers this software (or platform) to you as a service.

In the new world of cloud, there is no room to come down to. No one to come and shout at. Exactly nothing anyone can do to "assist" bringing the service back up. There's only one thing you can do, let the users know there's a problem and that it's in hand, and then sit on your hands. This can be incredibly disconcerting, for both you and the business. All of a sudden, it's no longer a question of who shouts the loudest. Services will be brought back online, as quickly as possible, in the best way, technically. If SLAs are breached, you'll get credits back. No consequential losses, no punitive damages.

Whilst this can be off-putting and indeed scary in some situations, there are naturally positives. When things go down, it's stressful. Majorly stressful. We've all been there late at night or over a weekend battling to get something back online. It's not something you'd wish on your worst enemy. It's not something you'll miss.

Whilst you may not think you are personally "important" any more, you're actually part of something much more important, part of a much bigger collective. You're one of millions upon millions of users getting very grumpy, very quickly. There's nothing like a service that caters to millions of users to get the attention, quickly, of vendors. When things do (rarely) go down, they tend to come back up very, very quickly.

You can of course mitigate some of these risks with a multi-cloud and multi-vendor approach, but you need to carefully consider the pros and cons of this approach. Is some downtime acceptable if it has significant savings in terms of cost and complexity, or must you push for that 100% SLA?

This change of relationship is a profound one. It is a change from a supplier/customer relationship to a partnership relationship. As you move to the cloud, your fate and your service provider's fate become intrinsically and thoroughly intertwined. Their success is your success, their failure is your failure. It's a momentous change, and one your need to be fundamentally and comprehensively prepared to accept. The buck no longer stops with you, it stops with them as well as you. Shared responsibility needs to be something you become fully immersed and expert in.

This new normal also needs to apply to service providers and consultancies.

Service Level Agreements

As you move from a traditional relationship to a partnership relationship, there are KPIs and measures that need to be put in place to govern this relationship. The service description and operating commercial agreement now become phenomenally important documents. They govern, to the very lowest level of detail, the gives and gets of the relationship. Of these terms, the service level agreement is the most important. It will say something like we commit to make available xyz service to you, for a minimum of 99.9x% of the time.

Your partnership depends on this key metric. It will govern what success looks like for your provider. At 99.9% that's about 45 minutes of downtime a month. At 99.99% it's about 4½ minutes a month. So long as service downtime doesn't exceed that, it's all good.

It's important to dig a little deeper in to these SLAs though. Different services have different SLAs. Office 365 maintains a 99.9% uptime guarantee. VMs in Azure have a 99.9% uptime guarantee, but this can be increased to 99.95% with an availability set and even 99.99% with two availability sets. Just to increase the complexity, SLAs typically interact with each other. If you have a load balancer with a 99.95% SLA in front of a VM with a 99.95% SLA, this is an effective SLA of only 99.9% (99.95% * 99.95% = 99.9%). You depend on both and each can go down .05% of the time, combining to a 0.1% downtime overall. It's vital that you understand these compounding SLAs, or at least understand the concept behind them, as you rate the commitments provided and operational delivery from your service provider.

Issues such as this need to guide your multi-region or potential multi-cloud strategy.

Support

Support is a broad concept and something we will dig into in more detail as part of service management, but at a high level it's something which is vitally important and something you need to plan for up front.

When something goes wrong, who is going to respond to it and how are they going to interact with the underlying service provider? What kinds of support does your service provider offer? Are there escalated tiers of support available to either you or to other providers you may choose to partner with?

Getting the support relationship right and defining it properly are key to the successful operation of your new cloud environment.

We cover many of these topics in more detail in the other chapters of this book but for the purposes of this strategy Chapter there are some high-level concepts to cover before we move on.

Firstly, you need a single owner for your service management layer. All the governance and service operations activities need to be with someone who has a holistic view of your world and who understands the business. You can outsource this but the arguments for bringing this in house are compelling.

This is the point of overall orchestration of all IT services to the business and in an ever more complex service model with multiple vendors and partner relationships you need an impartial overseer keeping everyone honest and representing the business primarily.

Secondly, you need to own your IT strategy. It is entirely appropriate to bring in external expertise in the form of advisors and consultants but the Enterprise Architecture function and the ultimate arbiter of the 1, 3 and 5-year plan should be an internal resource.

This person needs to be accountable to the CIO and therefore the business on the direction of travel for the organisation's consumption of IT services.

The EA / office of the CTO function should also be thinking of ways to open new revenue streams for the business by monetising data and services where possible.

Lastly, you should look to build a cohort of suppliers behind the scenes with specialist best of breed partners alongside partners who can provide scale where needed.

Many of the Global SI community are struggling to onboard cloud services as these services cannibalise existing revenue. They are, however, excellent at providing scale services like service desk and application support.

Lots of new cloud focused MSPs are now appearing that can be folded into your service model and will sit between you and the services and vendor management of your chosen cloud provider.

Chapter

9

Procurement and financial governance

The way to stop financial joy-riding is to arrest the chauffeur, not the automobile

Thomas Woodrow Wilson (United States President, 1856 – 1924)

Building a new procurement model

THE first step on a journey to a Cloud Operating Model is to build a model to support procuring your new cloud services.

Procurement and financial governance are radically different in a cloud world. In a cloud world, we are moving from purchasing assets, be they physical hardware or IP rights, to consuming services of varying descriptions. We are buying various levels of capability and offering based on very different pricing models.

To understand how to procure and govern these new cloud services you first must understand what it is you are buying and the metrics and measures which are used by each one.

Some of these models are based on a fixed price per unit / month (typically SaaS services). Many components include some level of variability (i.e. PaaS and IaaS services).

It's important as you start to build your procurement and financial controls, you build an ability to support variability. It is, as a rule, almost impossible to predict accurately exactly how much you will be spending monthly on your cloud services. Instead, think about how you can build a model which includes pre-defined, pre-authorised blocks of spending, with additional governance and controls if these are exceeded.

The next important question is where you are going to procure these cloud services from. Traditionally, you might have bought hardware and software from a reseller or distributor. In the case of Microsoft licencing, you might have bought them from a Licensing Service Provider (LSP), potentially as part of an Enterprise Agreement.

These licencing vehicles and partners play less of a role in this new cloud world for all but they very largest businesses. Instead, organisations like Microsoft have radically overhauled their licencing programs in a move to a more flexible, consumption-based model.

Cloud Solutions Providers (CSPs) who can combine licencing with professional and managed services will typically be the partners you will purchase your licences and cloud capacity from in the future. These partners will either source these licences and capacity directly from Microsoft (direct CSPs) or via distributors (indirect CSPs) before selling them on to you.

One of the advantages of a move to a cloud-based consumption model is clarity and transparency of pricing. One of the disadvantages of a move to a cloud-based consumption model is clarity and transparency. The price is the price which is the price. In the old world, RRPs were largely ignored as organisations cut specific deals with vendors. There were large discounts available in line with scale. If you wanted to buy Microsoft licencing, you were best to do it in June at the end of Microsoft's financial year.

Whilst there are still *some* discounts available to the very largest customers spending amounts in the millions of pounds per year, for the majority of customers these discounts and complex pricing models simply don't exist anymore. Simplicity is, in the case of cloud, the ultimate sophistication.

Procurement pipeline

To start your journey into cloud, you need to identify your strategic cloud provider and then put in a plan to onboard services. Typically, these onboarding services aren't delivered by the cloud provider themselves.

Many organisations, and presumably you if you are reading this book, have chosen Microsoft as your strategic partner. Congratulations, you made a good choice. If you're comfortable that Microsoft has ticked your various boxes and that you're good to go on Office 365 and/or Azure, crack on. Don't let a procurement pipeline get in the way of starting to use that right now.

There will, however, typically be a range of other SaaS solutions which you need to procure, and you need to build out a process to deal with this. The process won't be wildly dissimilar to the process you go through today to identify and procure traditional software. You'll need to go to market with your requirements and see who comes back with what. You might want a specialist business process automation solution, or an intelligent chatbot solution.

What's important now, though, is that whichever solutions you choose to onboard, that they sit within the realm of your COM. The questions you will ask of a SaaS vendor will be wildly different to the ones you will have asked to procure an on premises solution. You need to ensure that the platform their solution is built on will integrate with your environment. If you want to run it, as a service, without your environment you need to ensure it is compatible with Azure. You need to understand how it operates and how you will jointly support it with the vendor.

Getting this procurement pipeline right will mean you're best able to support your business units' requests for SaaS solutions which are a best fit for their requirements, whilst also ensuring they meet your availability requirements, that they're secure to your standards and that they work for you.

Financial Operation (FinOps)

We spoke about the difficulty in procuring cloud services because of the natural variability in the commercial models of different providers and services. This has introduced a whole new dimension to procurement and billing called FinOps or Financial Operations.

To horribly misquote Churchill, never in the history of IT has the power to spend so much rested in the hands of so few.

Each and every configuration change in cloud has a monetary impact and these take effect immediately a service is live and ready to use or immediately after it is shut down or resized.

This is not a negative thing. In fact, part of the power of public cloud comes from the fact you can, in near real time, manage the cost and benefit of your IT services, and even make these costs more transparent to the business.

The more traffic you send to a given service the more resource it can be allowed to consume.

Equally, as demand for services back off, these services can have resources removed thus reducing the run cost.

As an example of this, an early customer of Azure engaged a consultant to undertake an introduction to Azure workloads for their company.

The consultant arrived at the HPC (High Performance Computing) services topic just before lunch and kicked off the provisioning of a 50-node cluster as everyone filtered off to get some food.

When they got back 45 minutes later the environment had been provisioned, had burned through his free £120 MSDN of monthly Azure allowance he had access to, run out and shut everything down.

Operational Cost Governance

The simplest use case for illustrating the concept of managing cost as part of your operations ITOM layer is non-production workloads. These workloads rarely need to be on 24 x 7 and often can be off for extended periods of time.

If, for example, the release cycle for a given vendor supported application is quarterly, you may have a two-week period prior to release to production to allow for testing but for the rest of the time the test region for the service is idle.

If this service is switched off for idle periods, then the compute costs will be significantly reduced over time.

Another use case is workloads with variable, burstable usage patterns. If these are known and predictable then automated tasks can be carried out on the estate to both vertically and horizontally scale nodes and clusters.

In cases like retail where the burst can be an order of magnitude over the normal background run scale you can even architect a "stamp" type model which incorporates a full functional cross section of an application including presentation, application and database so even large-scale fluctuations can be incorporated.

Gone are the days when you need to scale your environment for peak demand, hope you get it right and then sit back and watch the environment tick over at 10% capacity for 10 months of the year.

If scale is less predictable and fluctuates over a day, then the concept of "autoscaling" can be investigated.

Autoscaling works very well in a cloud native architecture where each component is stateless and is designed to scale horizontally.

If your application is built to a microservices architecture and each microservice is in turn designed in this cloud native way you can set parameters within the cloud fabric to scale up and down based on the load on the service.

For heritage applications you can adopt a similar approach, but it is slightly less elegant due to the inherent lack of flexibility of the application architecture

If I use the example of a remote desktop service where you may have 10 session hosts to provide compute power to the user community consuming applications.

Without the use of complex tools, you would need to deploy all 10 nodes into public cloud, but you could shut 8 of them down to save the compute costs. You could then boot these servers on demand using the autoscaling feature when the load of the running nodes reaches a pre-defined threshold.

There are plenty of use cases for cost management that share a common theme and the ones that will be useful to your organisation will often be unique to you, your scale, geographic reach and so on.

Build and deploy governance

The second topic for consideration relating to financial governance is the concept of understanding and correctly allocating the cost of services at build time.

The issue at hand here is that as services are built by project services teams they begin to incur costs.

The concept of cost control and TCO for a given service is rarely front of mind for engineering resources during the implementation phase of a project.

Why have 4 cores on this server when 8 is clearly better. Why risk performance issues and rework by deploying a server with 16GB of RAM when the next one on the list has 56GB.

Worse still are developers who will think nothing of spinning up multiple nodes of whatever size feels right to test something then get distracted and leave them running for weeks unused.

As organisations begin this journey to cloud at scale, the need to address the financial governance topic will quickly bubble to the top of the list of priorities.

There are many ways of addressing this issue that will allow staff the flexibility to interact with cloud services as they need to while ensuring that someone, somewhere is making a conscious financial decision.

The structure of your public cloud environment plays into this. With Azure it is a combination of Subscriptions, resource groups and tagging along with careful consideration and application of role-based access and policies.

Although there are many similarities between organisations and their use of these features, the final position you take will depend on the size of the organisation, how many teams will be allowed access, your geographical reach and so on.

A small team within a single geography may well handle this governance at a team level and leave access to the management tooling largely open. A larger team with broad geographic spread or one with multiple operating companies with distributed management may well lock the management console down and limit interactions by delegation to a subscription, or resource group.

Wherever you sit on this continuum it is important you think this through before you commit to putting loads of workloads into public cloud.

Right Sizing and Optimisation

A final area for discussion on the topic of financial governance is one of workload optimisation.

Regardless of all the modelling you do you will be deploying workloads into cloud with a best guess. It may be a very informed and experienced guess and you may well get it very close much of the time but what you are unlikely to do is sit and watch your workloads over time to see if you can be more efficient.

Into this space drops specialist tooling. This tooling will keep watch of each of your virtual machines and PaaS workloads over time and will build a view of how busy they are and the resources they are consuming.

This tooling will compare these with the SKUs available to you and will make recommendations on changes you can make and the potential cost savings these changes will attract.

The more sophisticated of these tools will also allow you to apply personalised polices to this optimisation algorithm to limit recommendations you don't want.

Many of the public cloud vendors have a version of this capability baked in to the management portal. Microsoft purchased Cloudyn for this very reason and has made this available to customers through the Azure Portal.

There are other, third party tools in market that may give you a more granular estimate or may present the data in a way that is easier for you and your teams to consume. Some tools also have rich API capability, so you can use them to trigger run books or customised scripts if you want to automate some of this activity.

Alongside the optimisation tooling there is also the concept of reserved instances.

If you have a workload that will just be on all the time and you are comfortable you know the size of the VM is correct and is unlikely to change over time, you can purchase this as a reserved instance and attract up to 40% discount on the pay as you go pricing.

Chapter

10

Service management

If everyone is moving forward together, then success takes care of itself

Henry Ford (Industrialist, 1863 – 1947)

Building a new service model

S ERVICE management is the core of your Cloud Operating Model. It describes the actual nuts and bolts of how cloud will be born and be delivered inside your organisation. The service management that surrounds your cloud environment will dictate its success or failure. It's where the rubber meets the road in the intersection between agility and control. It's your front line in the border between the business and IT.

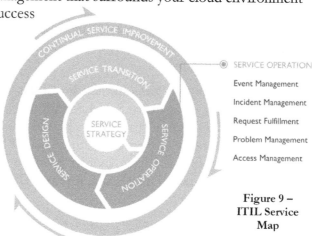

SERVICE OPERATION

Event Management

Incident Management

Request Fulfillment

Problem Management

Access Management

Figure 9 – ITIL Service Map

Service management within a traditional IT operating model is one of the best described and best designed set of standardised, off the shelf collateral available to organisations. Information Technology Infrastructure Library (ITIL) is in its third incarnation with another major revision due out soon. It describes end to end every aspect of IT service provision and how to model *and control* it.

More recently, Service Integration and Management (SIAM) has emerged as a useful construct to divide this service provision across multiple providers delivering different services with a single interface to the business.

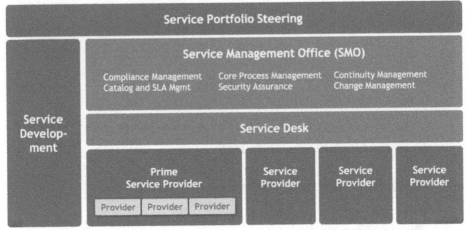

Figure 10 – Traditional SIAM Service Model © www.itforbusiness.org

These models are in extensive use today and are still even described as Future Operating Models (FOMs). Compared to what was typically in their place before, they were brilliant. They still offer a lot of value today. They were, however, a product of their time. And time moves on, fast.

Many organisations now feel suffocated with this siloed approach to IT delivery and accessibility. Standardisation necessarily delivers a lowest common denominator approach to IT capabilities. A service catalogue must support requesting a server in the same way as requesting a laptop, or a user having a problem accessing their email in the same way as being unable to run a CI deployment script.

Many cloud service lines now also cut across a number of their parent towers, such as datacentre and hosting in the example above. How do you deal with these new service lines? How can you present them up to the business with the best of what you do today, but a new level of flexibility and agility that the business require to effectively utilise the cloud?

These are some of the concepts that we explore within this chapter.

A tower or a bungalow?

If you operate with some form of SIAM model within your organisation, you'll be familiar with the concept of towers. Each describes a number of service lines and interfaces to the overarching SIAM owner. In a new world of cloud, these service lines will often be described differently and fail to sit neatly within the ontology your current model is built upon.

The primary difference between a traditional ITOM and a COM is the interrelationship between the business and these new cloud service lines. How do users provision them? How do they access them? How do they get support on them?

In a traditional ITOM, from a datacentre perspective, the server ruled the world. There are thousands of organisations with millions of example server definitions within their service catalogues. Do you want a blue one, 4 CPUs, 2 CPUs, how many disks, how much RAM? Once you've chosen your server, choose which environment you want it deployed into. Dev, UAT, Production? Pages and pages of options of configuration items (CIs) to deploy into and be managed within your organisation's ITOM.

In the new cloud world, especially in a cloud-native Gartner Mode 2 world, CIs become less and less important or relevant. The exact physical and virtual manifestation of an application at any given time of the day, week or month matters purely from a billing and monitoring perspective, not from a support or availability perspective. Environments become ephemeral, short-lived and capable of automatic recreation on the fly. Why have 3 environments for an application when you can have as many as you need, on any given day, dynamically, based on who was testing what part of the system?

The key to building a successful COM is to free it from the confines and control of a traditional ITOM, whilst still maintaining the security and policies that your organisation requires. The service line you're building has some similarities with a traditional tower forming part of a distributed service delivery model, but some very important differences. It needs to exhibit some of the same capabilities (such as SLA delivery) but can deliver this in much improved ways (such as real-time).

You may describe it as a bungalow. You may describe it as a naked service line (i.e. one without a parent tower). You need to agree how you see it internally, and how you will manage it. You probably won't know the answer to this question yet, but the more capabilities of the underlying cloud platforms you expose and the more you understand how users are consuming and demanding support on these capabilities, the clearer it will become to you. The *general* rule is, of course, the more you refine process the more agility you can deliver.

Service Portfolio Lead

One way, and arguably the best way, of moving your service provision on is to take a portfolio approach to your services as opposed to the service line concept.

Yes, you still have servers that need patching and monitoring, but you also have SQL Azure elastic pools and data factory instances. They will need monitoring also and possibly backing up depending on where and how they are used.

Your portfolio can be organised around function then applied to any number of cloud services. Monitoring can be a function. You need to consider how you will monitor an increasing number of cloud objects for uptime and telemetry.

Backup is another function and likewise you need to consider how to do this across all manner of services in cloud and on premises.

Non-data persistent services don't need to be maintained as they can often be recreated from scratch using scripts.

You also need a reactive function to handle incident management and a proactive function to do day to day administration.

Once you understand the landscape in relation to this functional view of service, you can then start working on automation.

Remember, the nirvana here is an architecture where you have a technology capability delivered with a single toolset trying to use cloud native services wherever possible.

Don't build file servers, use Azure Files. Don't build SQL server clusters if you don't need to, use SQL Azure databases. Don't host IIS on Virtual machines, use app services.

If you approach your portfolio in this way, then the business is free to deploy services at will consuming these services in a way that automatically inherit governance from your service management layer.

There is a need for caution here. Do not attempt to create a service portfolio that mirrors the Public cloud vendor's one. i.e. don't create your company's version of Azure files. The Microsoft one is fine. Let them use it but make sure you know how to manage it.

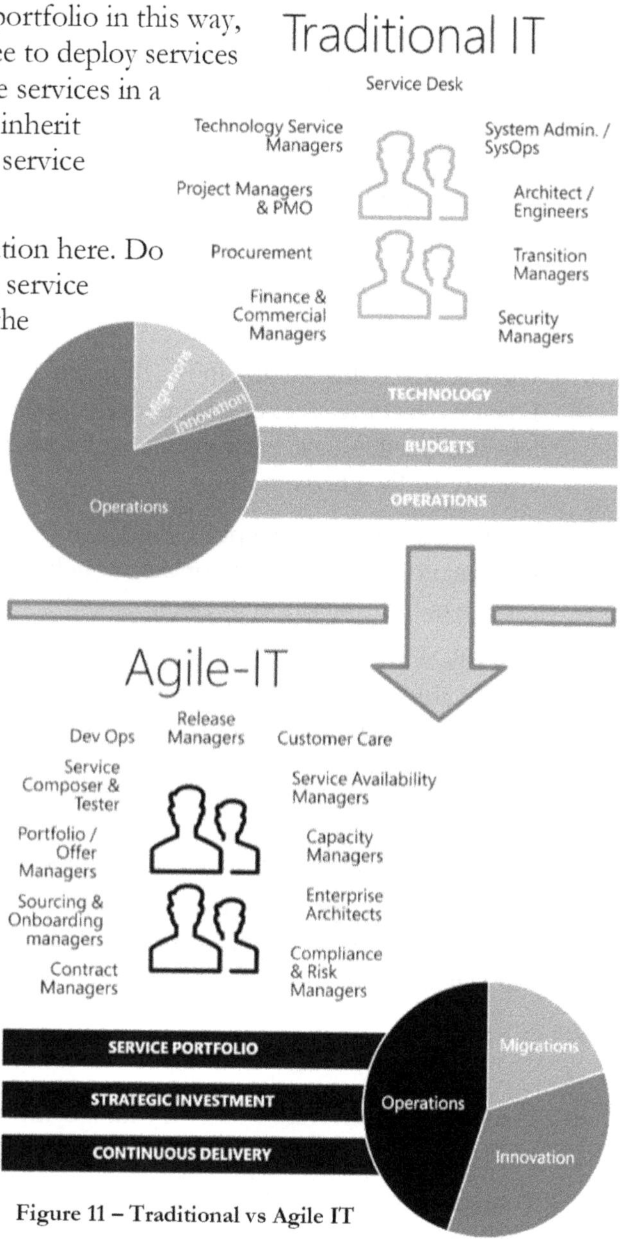

Incident

Incident management as a concept doesn't change a whole lot apart from the fact you can begin to automate certain things.

If you remain largely VM based in your first pass, this process will likely go to a server resolver team. This team will,

Figure 11 – Traditional vs Agile IT

however, need to also absorb the storage and networking elements as these components are abstracted into the VM configuration in the Azure portal.

The more you shift right in the maturity model, the more your incident management process will be dealing with code issues rather than infrastructure.

Again, the nirvana here is to try to automate incident resolution as much as you can. And, in the future, to use virtual engineers (bots and machine learning) to predict and avoid incidents. In a Mode 1 world incident management will still take a feed from an alerting platform and either invoke a run book or pass this alert on to a technician for resolution.

As you move towards Mode 2 we begin to see concepts like *immutable* environments. These can also be known as ephemeral environments.

We will cover this subject in much more detail in the Chapter on DevOps, but the essence of the idea is that is it easier, quicker and less risky to deploy a fresh instance of something rather than attempt to fix a broken one.

We have seen this concept in the desktop space for a while in organisations that have lite or zero touch Operating System Deployment to desktop devices.

Mix this with an application deployment toolset and no local user data as this is on OneDrive or an equivalent and you can just redeploy a desktop quicker than you can fix one.

Likewise, if you can deal with an application component failure by redeploying a fresh copy then this will have a fundamental impact to the way you deal with Incident management.

The ability to treat application components as immutable is directly related to the architecture. This in turn goes right back to your strategy and how serious you are about embracing cloud.

Change and risk

As with Incident management, Change and Risk management need to be reimagined in this new Operating Model of ours.

Change Management is probably the most impacted of the service management processes as you have to come to terms with the fact you no longer have full operational responsibility of the whole environment.

The move from build and run to consuming services is transformational to the change management process.

The underlying service fabric for many of your services is under constant change. You will have the ability to manage some. You will be told about some in time to prepare and there are some changes that just happen.

Microsoft is very good at sharing upcoming changes that they consider to be customer impacting.

An example of this will be a service going end of life or otherwise being deprecated. You often get several months' notice and a suggested upgrade or migration path.

Other changes to service like an uplift to mailbox sizing in Office 365 or the change of a licencing plan will often be circulated with the responsibility falling on the in-house IT team or service provider to keep up to date with these changes.

Changes to the underlying platform are not exposed and are run internally to the cloud hosting provider.

You will need to start to look at your environment in groups of services. Those services you control like your virtual machine guest operating systems, SQL servers and such like can be managed in a traditional sense.

Services you consume like Office 365 and PaaS services in Azure will need to be treated as third party and you will have little to no say over when changes take place. You will, however, be notified of these changes so you can handle the necessary communications to staff.

All of this we have covered so far is a challenging but achievable adjustment to your change process. What does this look like in a Mode 2 world?

In Mode 2 change is the whole point. The ability to make potentially thousands of micro changes a week is where you derive the business benefit that Mode 2 workloads deliver.

In this model you can't possibly hope to govern these workloads through a formal change process, so these workloads need to have strong testing and rollback baked into the deployment process.

Again, we cover this in more detail in the DevOps chapter but for now we will leave it that you will need to start educating the service organisation of where this cloud conversation is inevitably headed so they can start to get a feel for how this will look as you progress on your cloud adoption journey.

The new "run" business

Significant changes need to be made to your overall service management organisation to support this new world of change and automation. Barriers need to be broken down. Teams need to come together and collaborate more. New service façades on top of SaaS services need to be introduced. Platform services teams need to be born.

If we look at a traditional service such as email today, a simplified view of what your service management organisation might look something like this:

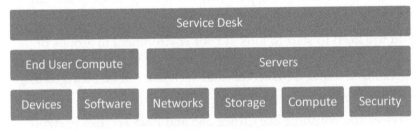

Figure 12 – Traditional support model

When we move to a service such as Office 365, your service management organisation needs to change to something like this:

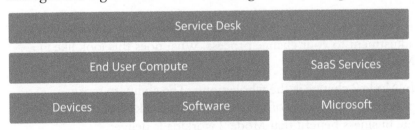

Figure 13 – SaaS support model

This simple change has profound impacts. As we discussed in chapter 8, there is now a symbiotic link between your service organisation and that of your new cloud provider. You no longer have access to server teams to diagnose and fix issues with the underlying infrastructure supporting your business. Your cloud provider now employs these people. What's important is the interface between you and them.

You may choose to interface directly with these providers, you may choose to work via a cloud solutions provider. However, you chose to solve this challenge, it will be regularly tested within the operation of your new run organisation. You need to ensure that you have access to the right people, as quickly as possible, with as tight SLAs as possible to deliver these new services to the users within your business.

The support model for internal line of business applications becomes even further removed from what it is today. Today, there is clear separation from the development/onboarding teams and the operations team, with defined hand-over mechanisms:

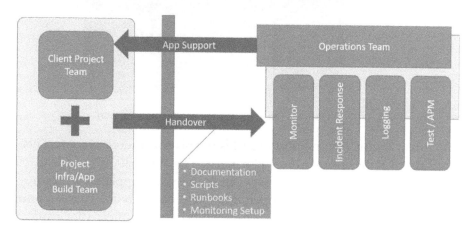

Figure 14 – Traditional application support model

This disjoined approach to application delivery has significant time implications. Typically, there can be a 4-6-week delay in getting an application from the project team to the operations team. When issues do appear, there is naturally somewhat of a "them and us" relationship between the two teams. Once the project team has delivered, they often disavow themselves from any issues in production. This only serves to increase the complexity of this handover as the operations team seek to turn every rock and fully satisfy themselves of the operational readiness of the application.

In the new run world, these teams collapse together. They become two sides of the same coin, working collaboratively together:

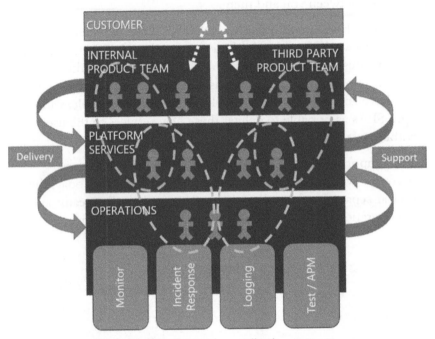

Figure 15 – Next generation applications support

Key to this new support model is the platform services team. This team is the special sauce. The ninjas. The automation specialists. The team that translates between the work the applications team is doing and the work the operations team needs to do. They support both internal applications teams and third-party ones. They work hand in glove between the two worlds.

There are two models that can be used when establishing the platform services team within your COM. There is the "centre of excellence" out model and the "community of practice" in approach. Both have had various levels of success in organisation today but deciding which model works for your organisation encompasses many different facets. You need to consider your funding models, the overall roles and responsibilities in your organisation and the DevOps principles that will mandate the reduction or removal of the silo.

For instance, if your organisation is much more product and green fields based, the development teams will most likely come together to build the services within the platform services team in a community of practice approach. They will complete the building of the new capability, ensure that it's productionised, ensure that the model is in place for what the developers will look after and what operations will be responsible for and then go back to their product teams.

Alternatively, you may have a large enterprise organisation with development or product teams who are more intent on laying out their requirements to operate and potentially provide team members on a more permanent basis to support the ongoing provision of services that they need in a centre of excellence style platform services team.

Roles and responsibilities

All of these fundamental changes to your service management organisation have to start from the top. They have to start from the beginning. As project/innovation and operations teams come closer and closer together, so do their reporting lines. Whilst digital initiatives within organisations often drive a lot of this change, they need to operate in lock-step with the operation's organisation. Ever heard the story of the digital team who have decreed "PaaS-first" and the operations team who don't officially support PaaS in production? You see it time and time again. Two poles pulling in opposite directions. Two separate organisations bereft of a common strategy or goal.

If you want to get your service management organisation firing on all cylinders and adequately supporting the business, you need to dissolve the fiefdoms. Everyone needs to be on the same page, inside the same organisation.

There are many approaches to achieve this goal, but the simplest is to at least make sure everyone shares the same reporting lines. There are many roles which can perform this function. A chief information officer (CIO), chief technology officer (CTO), head of digital (HOD). It doesn't matter what you call this person. If you really want to become truly digital, what matters is that they head a joint organisation and that they work to ensure that the distinct parts of the business play nicely and work together.

Chapter 11

Access control, security and provisioning

The need for security often kills the quest for innovation

Haresh Sippy (Industrialist, 1946 –)

Rethinking your attitude to risk

S ECURITY, security, security. Never has one word struck so much fear in to the minds of CIOs, CEOs and boards of directors. It's a trump card that can be played in an almost arbitrary way, in any given situation, to typically achieve the wrong result. We can't do this. Why? Security. We can't do that. Why? Security. Where this is ever any overlap between security and innovation, security wins.

Security is, of course, incredibly important. You only need to watch the news to hear about the latest data breach, the latest ransomware, the latest exploit discovered within something you use every day. In the words of James Rozoff, although *"Security is an illusion … it is a pleasant one."* Security, ultimately, is about risk management. What level of risk are you prepared to take as an organisation? What odds are you prepared to place a bet on? A one in a million chance of something happening, or a one in a several billion? What damage might arise from this theoretical threat we are protecting against?

For many years, security was the main reason organisations gave for their failure to adopt public cloud services. We can't use service x,y,z because *"[insert some reason related to security]"*. Over recent years, most of this fear, uncertainty and doubt (FUD) has melted away, and many now openly admit that the security delivered by most of public cloud providers is actually far in excess of the security that can be delivered on premises. Many still don't and still subscribe to the cloud-is-not-secure mantra. To those readers, you can stop reading here. We wish you good luck.

If you're willing to believe and you now want to understand how to take advantage of the security that is on offer from the public cloud, in this chapter we will explore what you need to think and about and the questions you need to ask to ensure what you deliver is at least as secure as what you do today, and more likely, more so.

Access Control

If access control = authentication + authorisation, or put simply, who are you and what are you allowed to do, identity is the most important ingredient in the recipe.

Identity as your chain of command

A central part of any COM is the definition and implementation of a cloud identity provider (IdP). Your operating model necessarily depends, at every single point and in every single scenario, on the system identifying who you are and/or what group of users you belong to.

In the on premises world, almost exclusively, Active Directory is this source of this identity. Every user and every service has an Active Directory credential. In the cloud, you need an equivalent of Active Directory, but instead of just authenticating and authorising access to devices and legacy applications, a cloud identity is used to control access to cloud platforms and services. A cloud IdP is a single sign-on (SSO) platform on steroids.

There are a number of cloud IdPs on the market today, including Okta, Auth0, Centrify and Azure Active Directory. Each has pros and cons and an associated commercial model. Most deliver some form of Active Directory federation. The first thing you need to do is undertake an evaluation of these IdP platforms, look at what they support, ask the smart questions, make a choice on the one that will work for you and then get on and deploy it. As quickly as you can.

Deploying a cloud IdP can be straightforward. It can be complicated. If you're linking it to your existing on premises Active Directory there may be additional work you need to do to tidy up your current environment. You might not have followed best practice. Your environment might have evolved over time. You might have acquired or divested organisations which form part of your Active Directory forest but are not good neighbours.

Although sometimes daunting, it's necessary work as your identity model forms the core of your COM. Take the time to do it right. The good news for Office 365 users is, you already have a cloud IdP. You may not realise it, but the page you log on to Office 365 with is in fact Azure Active Directory.

Multi-factor authentication

Once you have established your IdP, you need to start to build the controls which surround it. Whilst multi-factor authentication (MFA) was the preserve of the biggest and most security-paranoid organisations in the past, with the cloud, this capability has been democratised to all. There is no longer a requirement for expensive hardware access tokens or proprietary solutions. It's typically built in, out of the box. You now have the choice of whether to roll it out to all, to a subset of users, or based on a given set of criteria, for example whether the user is at home or work or whether suspicious activity has been detected. Agree your rules and incorporate these into your COM.

Single sign-on

In the same way that MFA was the exception rather than the rule of thumb, the same is true of single sign-on. It used to be a nice-to-have. Something you did if it wasn't excruciatingly difficult or expensive to do. Within a COM, it's a virtual necessity.

We discussed earlier the requirements you place on service providers as part of a procurement exercise, and SSO support should clearly be a major factor in your decision-making process. With the proliferation of SSO standards, such as OAuth, finding a service provider who can participate within your identity realm is relatively straightforward.

Many cloud IdPs have support for hundreds if not thousands of pre-built integrations. At the time of writing, Azure Active Directory supports more than 2,500 SaaS-based applications.

Joiners, movers and leavers

JML is an important process to introduce into your COM. A joiners, movers and leavers process describe the steps that you take when new employees start at your organisation, change role or depart. There are naturally a series of very serious security implications to people being given access to systems, changing access, or having that access withdrawn.

The work involved in this process depends on the kinds of cloud services and cloud IdP you are using, along with the setup of your single sign-on access to each one of these systems. Typically, single sign-on is based on identity federation and a token-based chain of control. A target system uses your main credentials to provide access. For these services, your JML process will be fairly streamlined and will rely on simply creating or disabling a user account within either your on premises Active Directory or directly within your cloud IdP. Users can be moved into, out of or between security groups to control access to differing systems, in the same way as you typically do it on premises today.

In some scenarios, relying services have their own, independent instance of a user's identity which is piggy-backed on to the main credential. Enabling or disabling a user's primary credential doesn't necessarily enable or disable the secondary account. Moving a user between security groups might not modify their access within these systems. For these scenarios and systems, you will probably need to increase the complexity and tooling that your JML process leverages. Suitable technologies include Microsoft Identity Manager (MIM) and others. Azure Active Directory Premium (AADP) also has prebuilt functionality to achieve this for cloud services such as Workday.

Best practice for your cloud IdP

Once you have your cloud IdP enabled and deployed and your users synced with it, you can start enabling federated access to your cloud services, such as Office 365 and Azure. The best practices you have leveraged on premises for years apply just as well in the cloud. Concepts such as always using security groups rather than individual users to setup access to operations within the cloud environments. Leveraging inheritance and hierarchies, for example starting with a broader definition of users, narrowing down and down as your get more specific with the users and the kinds of operations you want to allow. These concepts are the same in the cloud and should be the same in your COM.

IdP and your cloud platform

For SaaS applications, your identity model will be relatively straightforward and will broadly mirror how users are provided access to on premises applications today. For your cloud platform (IaaS/PaaS) the complexity increases somewhat.

Your IaaS and PaaS layers will contain the actual nuts and bolts of your underlying applications, the servers and services which compose them. You will typically have multiple environments for each of your applications, including test/dev, UAT and production. Differing user access rights will apply to each one of these different environments and sets of services.

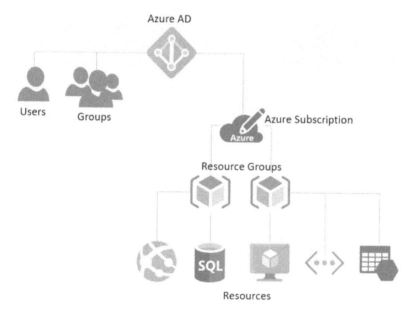

Figure 16 – Azure security model

The concept of an environment may also change. With traditional infrastructure, you have a given set of pre-provisioned environments which are set up in advance and in to which servers and security groups are deployed. You will still have these kinds of environments in the cloud, but you may also introduce ephemeral environments. An ephemeral environment is one which is created and destroyed on the fly, often at a high rate. The environment will be declarative, or in other words self-describing and encapsulated. It will be based on a set of templates and scripts which can be automatically deployed. An application won't be deployed in to *the* given environment, instead a *new* test and dev, UAT or production environment will be created, on the fly, specifically for *this* application. It's a very different concept.

What makes up an environment may also be different in this new cloud world. Traditionally, an environment might include a large set of assets, including servers, networks, VLANs, switches and so on. In the new cloud world, an environment might just be a specifically defined group of services, such as a resource group.

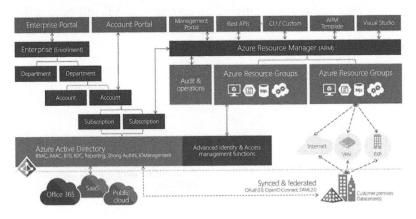

Figure 17 – Azure role-based access hierarchy

However, your environments are being deployed, you need to make sure you have sufficient identity controls to secure and manage them. Typically, owners and a set of differing roles beneath them.

Security

The security of your cloud environment is naturally an all-encompassing and broad topic to discuss. Your approach to security is something that will involve several individuals and teams from across your organisation.

Typical security covers physical, infrastructure, networks and VM/apps. By moving to the cloud, you no longer need to focus on the physical and infrastructure layers and can instead focus your efforts on the network and VM/app layer. Whilst your specific security design will not necessarily form part of your COM, the principles and vendor solutions (native vs third party) you will enforce do need to be agreed and planned as part of your COM as they will have far-reaching implications for things such as support performance and availability.

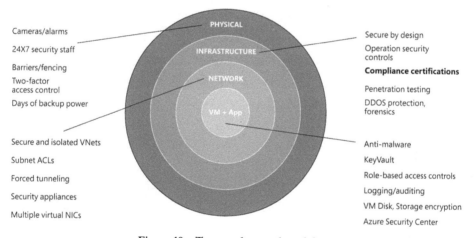

Figure 18 – Trust and control model

Perimeter security

As with a traditional on premises environment, the first thing you need to protect is your perimeter. Azure contains several capabilities built natively in to the platform to help meet this demand for perimeter security, including Azure's DDoS Protection and Mitigation service and its Firewall service.

There are also several third-party security products available on the Azure marketplace, including Palo Alto, Barracuda, Checkpoint and more. These third-party appliances are particularly useful when designing a hybrid perimeter security model and you have physical or virtual appliances from these vendors deployed on premises today. In this model, Azure becomes just another datacentre with ingress and egress points which need to be protected.

Customers who have deployed ExpressRoute have additional options and requirements for their Azure environments. An ExpressRoute circuit is a private link between the Microsoft datacentre(s) and your existing offices and datacentres. Some customers chose to route all their traffic in to or out from Azure and Office 365 via this connection. This way, all traffic can be inspected on premises via an appliance, other than certain whitelisted internet services such as Windows Update.

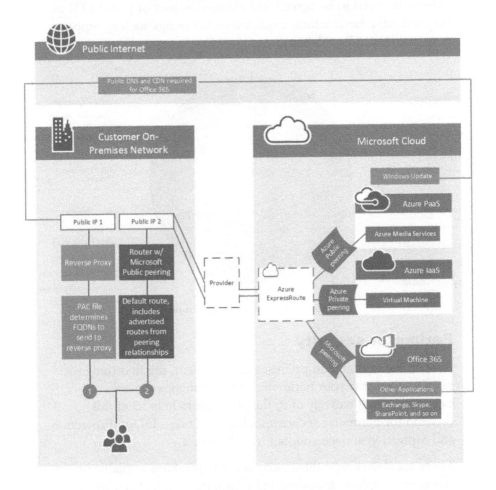

Figure 19 – Azure ExpressRoute conceptual diagram

Leveraging ExpressRoute and forced tunnelling can have significant impact on your available bandwidth and network capacity and is something that should be carefully considered.

Where you are exposing web applications to the internet, directly from inside Azure, you will also need to deploy a web application firewall (WAF). A WAF moves beyond the capabilities delivered by a standard firewall (can I connect on this port) to understanding the detail of web traffic and inspecting it to look for inappropriate behaviours and attacks by malicious third parties. They protect against common attack vectors such as SQL injection attacks.

Historically, dedicated web application firewalls were expensive to procure and to configure. In Azure, they are even simpler than deploying a VM. Azure has its own WAF capability inbuilt, or there are third parties which also have solutions available out of the box. Both allow extensive configuration and control of web traffic entering your environment.

Internal security

Once your perimeter security is in place, the next thing you need to ensure is that you enforce appropriate separation of network segments internally. This is something you may have done using VLANs or enforcing security between different subnets. In the cloud, this still what you do, you just have a different set of tools and services to achieve it. Instead of VLANs, in Azure we have virtual networks. Each virtual network is assigned a pool of IP addresses and a set of routes and connections through to other virtual networks. In the same way as you might have set ACLs on a firewall to control traffic between network segments, in Azure you set network security groups. These NSGs can either be applied to VNETs or to resources which attach to a virtual network.

Some organisations choose to deploy third party appliances to control this flow of traffic between virtual networks in the same way as they control ingress and egress from a cloud environment. Others choose to use native capabilities.

VMs and apps

Security at the VM and application layer is a complex and in-depth topic in its own right. Each application will present a bespoke requirement for connectivity and the approach you take to secure each one will be different.

Again though, the major topic for your COM is not the specifics, but to define your overall approach to securing your VMs and applications. Many organisations take a move to the cloud as an opportunity to apply additional controls which they might not have been able or willing to apply before. These might include:

- Host based security / firewalls
- Enforcing IPSEC-based connections to VMs
- Deploying advanced antivirus and host-based intrusion detection

Whilst your COM doesn't necessarily need to get into the details of exactly what you do on a VM by VM or app by app basis, it does need to include some high-level objectives and controls that you would like to be introduced, which leads neatly into the next chapter on monitoring, management and automation.

Azure Security Center

So, you've followed best practice and baked security into every part of your Azure environment. How do you police this and check your environment is configured correctly? The answer is Azure Security Center (ASC). Despite being a cloud service, ASC can provide visibility across your entire hybrid estate. It can help manage policy compliance, perform security assessments along with making proactive recommendations for issues to address and resolve. Investigate how you can leverage these capabilities as part of your COM.

Microsoft Threat Protection

Along with work you need to do specifically on securing your new Azure datacentre, there are a range of other tools and capabilities to help secure your end-to-end Microsoft cloud environment. One of the newest tools announced is Microsoft Threat Protection (MTP). MTP is designed to provide a view of an organisation's overall threat landscape so that administrators can easily spot new threats and attacks. Microsoft Threat Protection pulls data from Office 365 Threat Intelligence, Azure Active Directory Identity Protection, and Windows Advanced Threat Protection and combine them into one centralised dash board.

The piece particularly interesting about Microsoft Threat Protection is the sophistication of the artificial intelligence baked in to it, allowing new and unseen threats to be spotted and stopped in real time. Embedding MTP as part of your COM will provide you additional security and assurance around your Microsoft cloud environment.

Provisioning

Once your identity system is in place and you have defined your requirements and tooling for security, it's time to light up your environment and start giving users access. It's time to start designing and building your provisioning solution.

Designing your front door

Deciding how your users get access to a cloud environment is one of the most contentious and debated parts of COMs.

One of the defining characteristics of cloud is that it is automated and self-service. This is true. Rampant, uncontrolled and unabated access directly to the underlying cloud environment though is the stuff of nightmares to many others. How are we going to control this? How are we going to secure this? How are we going to financially account for this?

Provisioning is the tip of the arrow when it comes to the eternal agility vs control conundrum. We want to provide users quick and simple access, but we need to do it in a way where we can still enforce policy and governance.

Service catalogue

In a pure ITIL-based view of the world, the only entry point to consume services is the service catalogue. ITIL describes a model of defining each of the services which users can consume and giving them a shop window to provision these from. Want a VM? Sure, select one of the options below. Want a database? No problem we have these available to you. The service catalogue can define workflows, scripts, approval steps, everything a user could ever want with varying degrees of automation behind the scenes. Sounds perfect, right? Well, not quite.

Service catalogues can still play an interesting and important part of your cloud provisioning process. However, the sheer volume of items available to provision within a platform such as Azure makes them incredibly unwieldy. Consider for a start there are over 200 Azure services[33]. Then consider for each of these, there could be several dozen variants and options. For VMs alone (one of the Azure services), there are more than 150 different VM ranges and sizes to choose from[34]. Over 150! Every week a new VM size is launched and every few months a brand-new range comes online as hardware is physically deployed in the datacentres. Each type of VM has specific rules on what disks, networks or other services it can attach or connect to. Trying to maintain a mapping between your own service catalogue and the underlying platform is like bailing out an ocean with a bucket. It is possible, given enough time and enough resource, but it is about as close to impossible as you can get. It is also a never-ending job, assuming you were ever able to actually map the range of services available and create deployment scripts for each, by the time you had finished half would be out of date.

One of the other challenges to a service catalogue-based provisioning approach is that it typically flies in the face of the automation that the cloud delivers. A service catalogue is typically a web-based experience where a user searches for an item and deploys it. When your application is comprised of lots and lots of different items, VMs, databases etc, it becomes a boring and laborious task to sit there and deploy them one by one, to each environment.

Some organisations do, however, choose to make a small selection of configuration items available for deployment via a service catalogue. Perhaps a dozen VMs. A couple of database SKUs. A few easy-to-consume items to get less technically savvy users up and running on the platform before they get introduced to the wonders of templates and automation.

Cloud environments

Regardless of whether you choose to utilise a service catalogue, you need somewhere to deploy items in to. As discussed within the access control section above, you need to introduce some concept of an environment where users are authorised to deploy services in

---

[33] *https://azure.microsoft.com/en-gb/services/*
[34] *https://docs.microsoft.com/en-us/azure/virtual-machines/windows/sizes*

to. You need to come up with some name for them. You need to introduce the ability to create them. You need to introduce governance around them.

This is a useful place to interact with your service catalogue. Rather than having individual configuration items within your service catalogue, you can simply allow users to provision cloud environments instead. As part of the provisioning process you collect information from the user such as:

- Details of owner
- The project code
- The cost code
- Information security classification of the data contained within it
- The service wrap / operational requirements for the environment
- Other pertinent information

This information can then be used to automatically deploy the cloud environment. It can be used to set-up the access control to the environment. It can be used to deploy specific policies on to the environment, such as tagging and cost allocation.

There are several ways to achieve the automatic deployment of these environments. Some organisations choose to treat an environment as a resource group and set up policy and access control accordingly. Others choose to deploy a complete Azure subscription. There are a few factors to consider as part of this decision, but the most important is to agree the information you will collect and the mechanism to deploy the environment.

Once you have an ability to provision environments and provide access to your end users, you need to move to the next stage, managing them.

Policy and governance

Tying all of this together is policy. Policy is the mechanism you use to both control and also to enforce the provisioning and ongoing security and management of resources within your environment. Policies allow you to define what good looks like. What settings, configuration, placement and a raft of other rules apply to your cloud(s). Some of these policies will be simple to conceive.

- I want all of my data stored within the European Union. Or maybe specifically England.
- I want all data to be encrypted at rest.
- I must be able to allocate usage charges to departments/cost codes.

Some will be more complex. If this and this and this are true, I want you to do this, so long as something else is not true, in which case I want you to do that.

Policies should, wherever possible, align directly to security requirements. Policies should also, wherever possible, match external security standards, such as PCI DSS. In this way, you can demonstrate security compliance through policy compliance.

Your security teams also need to start thinking about the world through the lens of policy. Rather than theoretical rules about what can and can't be done, find the underlying controls you need to enforce and define it within policy.

Azure has extensive support for policies through Azure Policy. Azure Policy allows you to define complex sets of rules which can be enforced at both provisioning time and ongoing. They can define that, for instance, any VM being placed into any given environment should have certain agents deployed and configured. They can define that transparent data encryption be enabled for any SQL Azure instance.

Azure also has extensive additional capabilities provided by Desired State Config (DSC). This allows detailed configuration patterns to be attached to Azure services to configure them on deployment and to maintain compliance with the configuration over time. Popular open source solutions such as Chef, Puppet and Ansible are also available within your Azure environment for organisations that make extensive use of open source platforms. Also check out the newly released Azure Deployment Manager.

Third party products also exist in this space which can span multiple clouds. These products allow you to set a series of policies which can be applied to environments after the fact. They support a variety of external standards and have already done the mapping as to what features and capabilities you need to enable on the underlying platforms to achieve them. You might already have an environment where you hadn't deployed Azure Policy or DSC and want to bring your environment into compliance. You might not want rigid policies and allow developers greater freedom but have guardrails in place to keep them on the straight and narrow. You might run other products as well as inbuilt capabilities to enforce and then independently demonstrate compliance.

Whatever approach you take to policy, make it your central platform. Make it the single point of authority. Keep it as fully managed source code within your software development platform. Covet it. Nurture it. It's now the front line between you and the bad guys and girls. You need it and you need it to work

Chapter

Monitoring, management and automation

The first rule of any technology used in a business is that automation applied to an efficient operation will magnify the efficiency. The second is that automation applied to an inefficient operation will magnify the inefficiency.

Bill Gates (Founder Microsoft Corporation, 1955 –)

IF we have not landed the message strong enough yet in this book, public cloud is all about automation. It would not be overstating it to say it is probably the leading differentiator between it and all of the alternatives.

The software defined nature of a public cloud fabric allows for many situations where you can programmatically instruct the fabric to perform a task via an API call from anywhere at anytime.

This brings a certain level of efficiency to the delivery of services to public cloud but by far the area most impacted by potential for automation is the operations function.

It should be the aim of all businesses ultimately to run as much of their IT operations using tools rather than people, freeing those staff members up to add value higher up the business value chain.

We have referred several times to the Gartner concepts of Mode 1 and Mode 2. With public cloud, we also have the ability to meet somewhere in the middle with a kind of Mode 1.5 where you can automate the management of Mode 1 workloads in something approaching a pseudo Mode 2 manner.

To put it simply, you don't necessarily need to transform your workloads to transform your service management function.

Clearly, the more cloud native a workload is the easier it is to apply sophisticated automation to it. We will be talking at length about this in the chapter on DevOps and will revisit these concepts of monitoring and automation in this new Mode 2 paradigm.

For now, we will look at how this applies to Mode 1 workloads and how you can begin to move towards a cloud native Operating Model.

More traditional workloads such as COTS applications installed and running on Virtual Machines in public cloud can also benefit from the type of automated processes cloud can provide.

To illustrate this let's take a fairly simple three tier application. Our fictitious application has a presentation layer on a web service running on server A, an application layer with some functional binaries that do "a thing" on server B and a database on server C.

Using cloud-based monitoring tools you can monitor for the health of the guest operating system and the primary workload running on each server's guest operating system.

In addition to this you can also get telemetry from the Azure fabric for the services you are consuming to run these virtual machines.

The compute object, the storage account, the end point, the network card and so on. This information from the Azure fabric can be blended with the log information coming from the guest operating system giving you a good understanding of the state of the component parts. Microsoft provides tools such as Application insights, log analytics and Service map and you can stitch together these components into a single application level view of health.

Now, we can imagine a situation where a component is in trouble or the guest operating system is throwing warnings out.

With log analytics you can create alerts that query the log data and can in turn trigger automated run books in Azure that can execute commands on the fabric and the guest operating system as required.

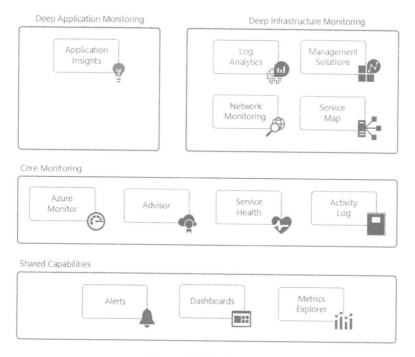

Figure 20 – Monitoring map

The ability to script almost any conceivable configuration change on both the public cloud fabric and the guest operating system has opened the doors to a whole new world of support options.

Monitor / Signal / Telemetry

Whatever you choose to call this function it is essentially the ability to use tools to look, often at great detail, at the health and performance characteristics of IT components and to report on or act upon this data in real time.

In our experience in working with customers in this space, the amount of monitoring capability deployed and its relative maturity in organisations is wildly diverse.

Many organisations have little to no monitoring or may have deployed some vendor specific tools discreetly into an area like a Storage Array or a Network.

Others have attempted a deployment of one of many popular tools to converge this function into a single place but have discovered, often quickly, that this is surprisingly complex and can take a huge amount of work before any perceived benefit is realised.

Other organisations have successfully deployed this tooling and are reaping the benefits of it but rarely does this toolset get deployed across all IT services and applications in a way that can provide a holistic approach to monitoring and alerting.

Where you sit on this continuum can be a leading indicator to your appetite for tooling and automation.

Another related topic is the toolsets themselves.

For many years, vendors have attempted to build products that do as much as they can squeeze into one tool. In some ways they have been successful and many of the market leading tools are very good at providing this "single pane of glass" view of your estate. We have used Microsoft System Centre Operations Manager for years in our services business to great effect.

The other approach is to deploy a mix of best of breed or vendor specific tooling to meet the same end.

There are pros and cons to both approaches but regardless we will refer to this as a management tool chain, a term that will mean more once you get to the chapter on DevOps.

As you move to cloud it is important that you consider this tooling in light of the cloud services you are likely to consume. In the short term these will likely be virtual machines and if you have any, your current tooling will adapt, but once you start to consume cloud native services your chosen tool will need to be able to cope with these too.

As you would expect, the direction of travel in this space is for cloud-based tooling managing cloud-based services.

Although System Centre is still a strong candidate in the Microsoft product set, Azure has cloud-based equivalents of many of the functions System Centre provides.

These cloud-based products are not quite on feature parity with their on premises cousins, but this gap is closing, and it may well be the better option to default to these newer tools even if you have to suffer a temporary drop in features.

If you are new to this tooling conversation you are being gifted a relatively low cost and low complexity option to introduce these tools by enabling these services in your subscriptions and starting to work with them.

Alerting and triggers

Once you move past the tooling conversation you start to work with alerts.

An alert is when a given service breaches a defined threshold and the monitoring tool is told to act in some way.

These alerts can be simple metric-based counters like CPU, Memory and Disk usage or more complex like specific service faults.

It is even possible to get very sophisticated and map a higher-level service like an application to its component parts and understand the impact of a given component to the overall health of the system.

The power of the cloud-based tooling is the addition of services like best practice analysers and other tools that can help pinpoint issues based on regularly maintained libraries constantly checking logs and surfacing advice and guidance to a console.

Once you have your alerting working well you need to start thinking through what you do with these notifications.

Initially, you will almost certainly send these to staff to remedy. You will configure alerting paths to email or text people or to raise a ticket in your service management tool for a resolver team to deal with.

You may wish to put a screen up in a service team area with RAG status displayed for the components or applications in your estate and use this to drive activity. Nothing says urgent more than red indicators on a screen in the middle of a room.

The next logical step is then to see if you can take these alerts and apply some mechanism to address a problem by performing a task without bothering anyone unless you really have to.

Modern Management and Compliance

With the onset of Windows 10 and Windows Server 2016, Servers and Desktop are now designed with cloud in mind.

Microsoft now considers a cloud managed Windows 10 instance as "Windows as a Service" where they are able to take an element of control over the build, deploy and service motion of endpoints. This is achieved in part by ensuring a very high level of compatibility with older operating systems and by the new concept of Servicing Channels which control updates.

In today's modern cloud centric IT landscape, an end user can purchase a Windows 10 device, enrol it as part of the out of the box (OOB) experience, sign in with a set of corporate cloud credentials and have the device build itself to the corporate standard.

The Windows Autopilot program take this a step further by allowing companies to pre-enrol devices to force the OOB process to automatically join Azure AD and Intune.

Once in Intune, other policies and applications can be deployed and the Servicing Channel chosen.

As Intune is an always on, Internet facing service, every time a device connects to the Internet it will check in with Intune and policy or updates will be deployed.

Scripting

For those of us who have been around IT for a couple of decades, scripting was a way of life for the Unix / Linux team who lived in their BASH shell crafting scripts using, among many arcane commands, awk, grep and sed to do all manner of things.

With the introduction of PowerShell v1.0 in 2006, Microsoft brought to bear a Windows based scripting language that was an attempt to replicate this ability previously only enjoyed by the Unix sysadmins.

Now Windows based sysadmins could begin to automate repetitive tasks and could begin to assess or alter the configuration of servers and workstations without the need for tools or compiled code to expose this ability.

PowerShell went through several iterations which finally led to the decision to take it multi platform and open source in 2016.

When Microsoft developed the interfaces for both Azure and Office 365, it is no surprise they have built these on PowerShell thus giving the IT community a common language with which to administer everything from a Windows desktop client, a Server guest operating System, Back Office services like SQL server and Exchange and the cloud fabric these services run on if they are being consumed from Azure and Office 365.

Microsoft also adopted the use of JSON as a format for the transmission of data used to describe types and attributes of services in Azure.

The combination of a language like PowerShell where you can assess and change the configuration of items across the whole cloud service stack with a descriptor file using the JSON standard you can pretty much do anything you like without ever sitting at a graphical interface.

This approach is becoming the new normal.

Microsoft introduced the concept of a "core" server back in Windows Server 2008 where no Windows Explorer shell was installed, and all tasks were carried out using the Command Line Interface (CLI).

All server operating systems since have had this option and the Nano server option with 2016 can only be administered locally though PowerShell.

The further right you shift in the cloud maturity model and the closer to Mode 2 you get, the more Scripting is the only viable option to do work.

If you and your team don't script it is vital you learn this skill.

Once you get a library of scripts and are doing a good portion of the day to day administration using this technique, you will begin to see opportunities to run certain scripts based on input like time of day or when an event is triggered.

This is the essence of basic automation. The things you start with don't need to be fancy, but they do need to save you work.

Do you regularly refresh a test region with data from the production system prior to testing a release? Script it. Once you do this a couple of times you may take the next step and realise you don't even need the test system most of the time and can begin to look at automating the provisioning of this test region with a script also. You have now saved both time and money.

The convergence of development and infrastructure is happening and as you move along the cloud maturity model this will become more and more obvious.

Your infrastructure team will need to solve problems that developers solved years ago like where to store their scripts, so they are easy to get to and others can use them. They will need to work out how to maintain and publish these scripts.

There is a lot of sense in sharing code repositories from the developers with the infrastructure teams and if you make that next logical step you are that much closer to the Nirvana of DevOps.

Chapter

DevOps and application development

Every company needs to be a software company

Satya Nadella (Microsoft CEO, 1967 –)

WE dissected in detail within the business book the wave of digital disruption that is sweeping the world at present and the opportunities and threats that this presents. Technology has phenomenal power to disintermediate and radically transform different industries. We introduced the concept that every company has to be a software company, but what does this actually mean? How does a company become a software company? How do you place technology at the core of everything you do? Of course, there are a hundred answers to this question, but in this chapter, we tackle perhaps the most complex of these. How do you start to build a software development function within your business and within your overall Cloud Operating Model? How do you put processes and governance around what is fundamentally a fast moving, fast changing and highly creative discipline?

What is DevOps?

This perhaps is one of the most difficult definitions within your COM. There are entire books several times the size of this one which inspect, dissect and attempt to define this nebulous phrase. Is it a set of tooling? Is it a process? Is it a redefinition of roles and responsibilities? Is it a change in corporate culture? The answer is, all the above. It represents a paradigm shift in how you think about software engineering and operational management. A very simple definition is, how can you empower developers to produce high quality software, which solves real business challenges, and which can be automatically tested and deployed into a secure environment where end users can access it? There are, of course, several orders of magnitude of complexity surrounding each of these words, but as a concept it is simple. Developers write code. We need to test that code and we then need to deploy that code. Easy right? Not quite so easy, no.

The great war

If DevOps is what we want, what are we replacing? Grab your sandals, it's time to go tree hugging.

If we look at the typical software development lifecycle today, one of the biggest challenges we face is that there are multiple disciplines at play.

Developers write code. They understand code and object-oriented programming and abstraction and parallelisation and the vast array of tools and techniques to deliver the magic of software.

Operations folk deploy code. They understand servers and switches and security and load balancers and firewalls and all the components that software needs to live and run on.

Both are intrinsically important, and both are symbiotic. If business is from Mars and IT is from Venus, however, developers are from the Milky Way and operations are from another galaxy, far far away.

Not only are the two teams far removed intellectually, they are typically far removed physically and organisationally as well. Very often, they report into two completely different parts of the business.

And so, the great war has raged, since the dawn of IT time. Developers sniping at operations. Operations sniping at developers. Two sets of individuals symbiotically linked, yet in a constant state of tension and warfare. Frankly, it's a miracle today that anything gets deployed into production in many organisations. When it does though, it typically takes weeks or months of waiting, testing, deploying, fixing, re-deploying, waiting, testing and so on and so on. Everybody doing their job, the way they are supposed to be doing it and there is only one set of people who suffer. The business.

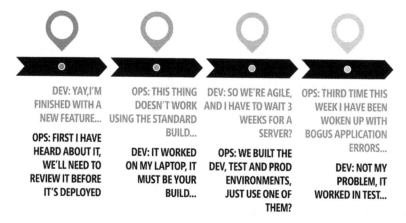

DEV: YAY, I'M FINISHED WITH A NEW FEATURE...

OPS: FIRST I HAVE HEARD ABOUT IT, WE'LL NEED TO REVIEW IT BEFORE IT'S DEPLOYED

OPS: THIS THING DOESN'T WORK USING THE STANDARD BUILD...

DEV: IT WORKED ON MY LAPTOP, IT MUST BE YOUR BUILD...

DEV: SO WE'RE AGILE, AND I HAVE TO WAIT 3 WEEKS FOR A SERVER?

OPS: WE BUILT THE DEV, TEST AND PROD ENVIRONMENTS, JUST USE ONE OF THEM?

OPS: THIRD TIME THIS WEEK I HAVE BEEN WOKEN UP WITH BOGUS APPLICATION ERRORS...

DEV: NOT MY PROBLEM, IT WORKED IN TEST...

Figure 21 – The DevOps problem statement

Restructuring your team

If developers and operations need to work seamlessly together in this new world, what does this mean to the way their teams are structured and how they collaborate?

The answer is, a lot. As we stated above, DevOps is not a thing in its own right. It is comprised of several initiatives, changes to the way people work and, most importantly, a change of culture. There can be no more them and us. There can be no more division and conflict.

Since the days of Patrick Debois (The Father of DevOps), coining the term at his first conference, organisations went about creating new silos of teams that would do both the dev and the ops, or somewhere in between and own the "pipeline" or delivery. This was precisely what Patrick was looking to avoid.

At the heart of the DevOps machine and culture movement is the quest to remove the number of handoffs between various teams and organisational structures required to complete a task, be it a dev task or an operational one. Building a team that sat in between caused the issue to become greater. In more modern DevOps practices, we've learnt that team responsibility needed to remain with the team that is best qualified and skilled. So how is the DevOps "team" established? It's about lowering the walls between the teams, providing a high level of communication, which requires a common language. Teams still own their respective areas of responsibility, but all teams have the ability to make change in all other verticals.

The best practice example of this is that of the glorious "firewall change". The development team may well require a port changed and not necessarily understand the implications of just opening up port 80 to the whole world from the database server. Rather than just asking the operations team to do it and have the proverbial fight that comes with that lack of understanding, the operational team allows the development team to see the infrastructure as code that wraps the security port protocols and allows the developer to "raise a pull request with the change". This gives the operations team two things. 1) the ability to explain to the development team why that may not be a good idea and what else needs to be considered or changed and 2) the ability to protect against the developer just making the change and causing issues. In reverse, the operational team may well look at the developer code or at least, process flow and see why they're trying to make a call on port 80 and then can talk to the developer about how the call can be made a different way.

Either way, that communication is the new "DevOps Team". Roles and responsibilities are respected, but hand-offs are reduced. If the port change was fine to make, the operations team would just click "go" and allow the roll out to occur... no questions asked.

There is no simpler practical step to this than a realignment of reporting structure. Today, operations typically report into some kind of head of operations. Development reports in to some kind of head of development and often these reporting lines don't converge until you get into the upper echelons of an organisation at some kind of directorial level. This doesn't work. Within a DevOps world, either developers need to report into operations, or operations need to report into development. Or better still, there is no more operations and developers, just a DevOps organisation that comprises of folks with a slant towards development and folks with a slant towards deployment and management. Some organisations completely drop the phrase "operations team" and rename these people site reliability engineers to demonstrate their role is now all about making code work effectively and efficiently in production, working hand-in-hand with developers.

The other substantial change to understand and act to achieve is a change in the roles of some of the people within each of these teams. Developers need to start thinking a bit more like operations folk and start to develop an understanding that they are not just writing code that will end up on some server somewhere that they have no appreciation of or care about. They now know their code will end up within some form of cloud service, probably chosen by either themselves or the architects within their team. They need to make sure their code is designed in such a way that it will seamlessly deploy into these services by respecting some form of service-oriented or micro-service-based architecture.

The bigger change is typically within the operations team. As we will explore below, along with the cultural changes and adaption in roles, the biggest change is the tooling and automation that DevOps necessitates. IT pros have been doing automation and scripting for many years, but in a DevOps world this takes on an ever more important part and becomes the *only* way that anything can ever be done. No more manual steps. No more workarounds. No more provisioning environments. *Everything* needs to be automated. Everything becomes templated. This may prove a big challenge to some team members who are used to doing things their way and are used to drawing low level infrastructure design documents. Some folks may not make it. Others will embrace and become excited about the power this level of automation can bring to the way they work.

Automation and tooling

So, you've fixed the culture, you've fixed the organisational structure, everyone is behind this new world and this new COM. What's next? Tooling.

Those of you that run a mature software development function will typically have some form of software development lifecycle management (SDLC) tooling. You may use TFS. You may use Jira. You may use several different tools. They probably work quite well and help you manage requirements capture and source control. Those functions remain and by and large remain unchanged within a DevOps landscape. What you need to add, typically, is continuous integration and continuous deployment (CI/CD).

There are, again, a vast variety of tools in this space and you may use some of them already. Azure DevOps (VSTS), Chef, Puppet, Ansible, Jenkins, TeamCity, Octopus. There are more tools than you can shake a stick at. Each has strengths, each has weaknesses. This book will not even attempt to delve into the details of how you set up an end-to-end CI/CD pipeline. How you inject security and "shift left" thinking. Which tool makes most sense based on what technologies your developers use and what technologies your operations team feel most comfortable supporting. This is a book in its own right and there are many in the market you can refer to. We will introduce you to some of the concepts to help you ask the smart questions about how you can introduce DevOps into your organisation.

Ultimately though, you need to do the research and make this tooling a central tenant of your COM. In a world of digital disruption and digital innovation your application development function becomes your powerhouse and giving teams access to the best tooling is the best way to help them be effective and deliver the right outcomes for the business. Get it right and you'll truly be able to deliver on the dream of rapid, agile delivery of software to your users and customers.

If you want to skip a step, however, and just make a simple choice for something that works quickly and simply out of the box, Azure DevOps is your answer.

Immutability

From the Latin, *"immutabilis"*. Unchangeable.

In the introduction, one of the most significant challenges we called out was the difficulty of supporting change within a traditional ITOM. Change is difficult. Change is dangerous. Change is something to be avoided. When we go deep under the covers though, we discover these statements typically only hold true because of one thing. They exist almost exclusively because of something called mutability.

You may remember something about mutable and immutable, maybe from a computer science class? It's a programming thing, right? Correct, but now it's an infrastructure thing as well. As infrastructure becomes programmable, so the concepts that apply to programming gain more relevance.

We've all experienced or heard stories before about bugs and defects that appear in production that weren't seen or couldn't be reproduced in UAT. The environments look exactly the same, yet somehow there is some tiny difference that you just can't quite track down. There goes your weekend.

In today's Mode 1 world, we have *mutable* instances of infrastructure. Ones we can mutate (change them). The most basic example of a mutation is patching. We don't rebuild a server from scratch each time a patch is released from an updated ISO which has the patch baked in. We patch, in place. Every time we install a patch or deploy an updated version of an application that runs on that server, though, we introduce tiny variants. Tiny variants between what may or may not have succeeded, at an MSI installer or DLL packager level, between one server and another given server which started out identical. If you update different configuration items stored on these machines enough times, bad config or defects can also creep in. Indeed, the vast majority of defects in production are due to bad config across environments.

Why do we do this then if it's so prone to error? It's because anything else is prohibitively expensive and complex. Building a server, however automated it is, takes time. It takes people. It takes coordination and approval. Applications consist of multiple servers, all of which need provisioning. Applications won't magically install themselves, someone has to do it. When you reinstall something, it typically breaks, at least 90% of the time.

Well, that used to be the case. But it's not the case anymore. The central concept behind cloud computing is infrastructure and application automation which delivers us the ability to leverage *immutable* environments. These are also known as ephemeral environments. Using Azure Resource Manager (ARM) templates and technologies such as Desired State Config (DSC) and Azure Deployment Manager, as an automation specialist, I can describe exactly what an instance of an application looks like. It doesn't matter how many servers and/or services it is comprised of. I can describe the components of the application and how each can scale up and down independently of the other components. I can also describe exactly how to deploy the application and configuration itself onto these underlying IaaS and PaaS services. I now no longer need to worry about patching (whether I'm using IaaS or PaaS), because at a moment's notice I can now recreate, from scratch, a completely new, ephemeral copy of my environment and application. That's game changing. It's also organisationally changing.

We spoke earlier about that changes that need to be made within your teams. Immutability is the central concept driving many of these requirements for change. We are no longer feeding and watering (administering) environments we provisioned historically. We are now scripting creating new ones. The more automated we can make the deployment, the better we can test it and the lower the likelihood of defects getting into production. That's why these new folks are typically called site reliability engineers. Their job is to stop defects getting into production.

I can't (typically) just take an application I have right now though and automagically make it support this new world. Infrastructure automation is very similar to software automation and development. It takes time. It requires new concepts to be introduced into existing architectures. Concepts such as stateless operation and centralised configuration. When we talk about applications which can exist in this new world, we typically talk about cloud native applications and almost invariably, these applications are immutable. Proper DevOps also required immutable environments which can be automated and deployed on demand.

Containers

To alleviate some of the challenges with IaaS-based deployments, containers have emerged over recent years offering some significant advantages.

A container is a bit like a virtual machine, but rather than containing an entire server operating system, it just contains the application files themselves. Multiple containers can then run inside a VM which includes the underlying operating system. Scaling up and down containers is quick and simple when compared to scaling up and down entire VMs. The industry standard container is Docker.

Containers by themselves are not especially helpful though. In the same way as you need something like Azure to automate and marshal the creation and destruction of VMs, you need the same for containers. You need high availability and fail-over between the underlying VMs. You need orchestration.

There are a number of open source container orchestration solutions in market, including DCOS and Docker Swarm. The newest entrant, which seems to be getting the most traction, is Kubernetes. Kubernetes originated from Google but is now widely adopted by all of the major cloud vendors. One of the founding architects of Kubernetes now works for Microsoft and under his guidance Microsoft released the Azure Kubernetes Service (AKS). This fully managed platform service automates and orchestrates all of the work involved in deploying and managing containers.

If you're more focused on .NET, you also have the Azure Service Fabric available to you. Service Fabric brings all of the capabilities of platforms such as Kubernetes, but also has significant additional capabilities beyond.

Platform services

Whilst many believe containers are the only way of designing and building modern applications, this is not necessarily true. One of the major advantages working with a cloud platform such as Azure is the availability of platform services, typically referred to as PaaS.

PaaS is a very different beast from infrastructure services or containers, even when you are leveraging immutability and automation. At a high level, PaaS services are a set of capabilities delivered by the underlying cloud service which can be consumed as services rather than delivered from servers you have to patch and maintain or containers you have to deploy and orchestrate. Rather than building an SQL server cluster, I can now consume SQL as a service and simply pay for the storage and performance requirements desired.

There are naturally pros and cons to any deployment method. The advantage of PaaS services is that users no longer need to main underlying servers or container orchestration platforms. The downside is users lose some of the control and customisation capable when you're in control of the end to end stack. Most platform services are themselves delivered under the covers by containers. SQL Azure is built on Service Fabric. App Service deploys IIS instances inside containers on top of VMs. The platform service is, in effect, a container orchestration service for specific containers designed and managed by the cloud vendor.

In a DevOps setting, PaaS services can have significant advantages. Provisioning PaaS services is exponentially more straightforward than automating the provisioning and configuration of VMs or containers programmatically. Users can instantiate a complete platform service with a handful of API calls rather than a complex set of deployment scripts. This makes creating immutable environments much more straightforward as users can create and tear down specific PaaS instances more easily than a set of VMs or containers which might support them.

Platform services can also be seamlessly scaled up and down based on performance metrics. How many transactions/messages/operations do I need to support per second/minute/hour? The pricing model also exactly reflects these performance-based characteristics. With a VM-centric view of the world I might not know if it was more CPU, RAM or disk performance which was required. You typically just scale up all of them.

There are hundreds of platform services on Azure covering data, messaging, media, device management, identity, security and much, much more. It's vital that you explore how PaaS services might benefit your developers and how they can streamline your application development workflow. Be bold. Mandate PaaS first.

Testing

Alongside immutability, a central tenant of DevOps is testing. Immutability specifically exists to aid, amongst other things, effective testing.

A key concept to understand is a failure model. There are two kinds of failure model. A deterministic one and a non-deterministic one. In laymen speak, a failure you can discover through effective testing and one which you cannot. The more wildcards you can remove from the equation (such as mutable environments or physical hardware), the more unexpected failures you can eliminate. Once we exist, as much as is possible, within a deterministic realm we can (in theory at least) remove all defects through effective, complete and automated testing.

Doing effective, complete and automated testing is no mean feat. We need to test *a lot* of stuff. We need to test code. We need to test logic. We need to test UIs. We need to test integrations. The primary reason to do testing is to fix things. So, we need to engage developers, at every stage. We need to shift-left.

"The term "shift left" refers to a practice in software development in which teams focus on quality, work on problem prevention instead of detection, and begin testing earlier than ever before. The goal is to increase quality, shorten long test cycles and reduce the possibility of unpleasant surprises at the end of the development cycle—or, worse, in production."[35]

In a shift-left world, we need to increase the lines of communications across the teams, and importantly between the automation specialists (ops) and the developers. The shorter we can get the feedback, the more quickly we can spot the defects and get them fixed.

In the first way, there was one-way communication from devs to ops. In the second way there is basic return of information from ops, but only in the third way can we truly shift-left when there is constant, automated and detailed communication between development and operations.

This might be immediate and interactive telemetry that a developer can access in development. It might be detailed stack trace information from an environment closer to production. It might be a Teams notification that a build has failed. The communication can come in lots of forms, but the easier it is for a developer to access this information, the quicker they can find the issue and the quicker they can fix it.

The testing we introduce therefore needs to be, in as much as possible, fully automated. We need to make extensive use of unit tests which can be executed and run at build time. We need to use ephemeral environments, so our end-to-end testing can run against exact replicas of what our environment will look like in production.

---

[35] *https://devops.com/devops-shift-left-avoid-failure/*

Figure 22 – The first, second and third way of communications

We need to knit testing deep into our software development and release cycle.

One of the reasons change has historically been dangerous is because it can introduce unexpected behaviour. If we can introduce thorough enough and automated enough testing, and we are only exposed, by and large, to deterministic failures, we can start to introduce change at a much faster clip. Without introducing additional risk. This is the raison d'être of Mode 2, cloud-native application development and delivery and key to your digital transformation. If you can be sure change isn't going to break it, you're building on solid foundations.

Pipelines

Pulling all these concepts together is the pipeline. A pipeline is the principal component of continuous integration and continuous deployment (CI/CD). It is a workflow. A set of instructions about the steps required to deploy an instance or a component of a given solution.

The first step is to take the source code from the version control repository. This code is then built according to the build scripts.

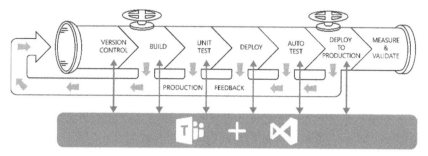

Figure 23 – A typical DevOps pipeline

Unit tests are then run within the compiled application and services. Assuming these pass, an instance of the application and/or services are deployed into an ephemeral environment. Further, automated integration and acceptance tests are run, before the environment is swapped/promoted into a production environment. Simple right?

Not quite so simple. The pipeline is the magic that holds the whole DevOps world together. It's the asset that delivers on the idea of reduced handoffs between teams. Depending on the complexity of your application, your pipeline might end up incredibly complex and elaborate. You will typically have multiple pipelines for multiple applications or multiple tiers within an application. Depending on the tooling you use, your pipeline might need to speak to a plethora of separate tools and processes. Anyone that has been involved in automation knows that to automate a manual process is several orders of magnitude more complex than you might imagine. Things always find a way of going wrong.

Once you can get your pipeline(s) working though, it's something to herald. It's the magic that allows you to increase your rate of change exponentially. Need to change something? Just modify the code, check it in, press a button and tada, it's in test. Press another button and tada it's in production. When you can do this, you embrace change rather than fearing it. Whilst you might not hit Amazon's million releases a year, even if you can do a release every week, or maybe even every day. That's huge progress for the vast majority of organisations.

Security

Security plays a very important part in this new DevOps world. Historically, security probably got involved reviewing low level designs. They may have asked for code drops to scan the source code. They probably enforced security software / patching schedules / penetration within production. It was a one-way conversation. We're going to tell you what to do, and once you comply we will allow things to happen.

In this new world, security can become embedded into the entire process end-to-end. Rather than stipulating requirements up-front, such as encryption at rest, security folk can now access the same deployment scripts and templates as developers. Security folks can modify these templates directly, enabling options and settings.

Security-related steps can also be inserted into the pipeline. The security movement within the DevOps methodology and mindset has grown to such a size that the term DevSecOps has emerged and entire organisations are being developed to purely tackle the automation that is security within the pipeline. Security used to be something designed at the beginning and validated at the end prior to the "go-live day", but we're now seeing organisations work to trust the pipeline over the end environments.

Automated code-scanning tools can check source code before it is built to look for vulnerabilities or bad code. If you're using containers, these containers can be scanned for viruses at the point they are created and sealed. You can then deploy as many instances of each container as you like, safe in the knowledge that each is virus free. You don't need to check your entire environment any more in production, just each of its building blocks at build time.

Monitoring

In the last chapter we explored some of the logging and monitoring tools available for your heritage estate. Depending on your application architecture, these tools also have applicability in this new world. We also have access to a range of other tools and services which are designed for a world of custom software engineering.

These tools capture additional metadata and telemetry which is not typically available to more infrastructure-focused tooling. Within Azure, Application Insights provides rich data about the functioning of applications, at the code, module or container level. How long does this call to the database take? What is the spin-up and spin down time of a container? What is the total number of individual transactions which make up my higher-level transactions (how many database calls per order for instance). Having deep visibility into the functioning of your application is vital to ensuring its health and optimising its cost footprint.

Figure 24 – Azure Application Insights

Chapter 14

The Technical Questions

Everyone hears only what he understands

Johann Wolfgang von Goethe (Writer, 1749-1832)

W E have outlined everything you need to think about as you start to build out your COM within the second volume of this book. As you have discovered, there is a lot to think about. In this second set of questions, we will enable you to dig even deeper. To start to position these challenges and decisions along the lines of a set of questions.

We have divided these questions into the same structure as the chapters within the second volume above. If you need some context around the questions, flick back to the chapter to which they refer to give yourself a quick reminder on the rationale of the question, or to help you best answer it.

You may not know the answers to every question. You might need to consult internally. You may to get help from your vendors or from a partner. Don't panic. This is a complex subject and answering all of the questions will take time.

1. **Section A** – Strategy and Service Providers
2. **Section B** – Procurement and Financial Governance
3. **Section C** – Service Management
4. **Section D** – Access Control, Security and Provisioning
5. **Section E** – Monitoring, Management and Automation
6. **Section F** – DevOps and Application Development

14.1 Strategy and Service Providers

Getting your cloud strategy right from the offset is the single most important factor which will determine the success, or otherwise, of your new COM.

In this chapter above, we discussed topics such as:

- Cloud strategy
- Multi cloud
- Hybrid cloud
- Your current estate
- Bimodal IT
- The relationship with your service providers
- Service level agreements and
- Support

We will now give you some questions to ask about these topics.

☒	Question	Why this matters
☐	14.1.1 How much does the business think IT can be used as a key differentiator in the market?	We discussed in great detail within the business volume how IT can be used a strategic differentiator. It's vital that the business accepts this is true. It's vital they accept the part you need to play within transforming the business.
☐	14.1.2 Has the business got clear and documented goals in the form of a business strategy with a 1, 3- and 5-year view?	This is a very important starting point. If the business is struggling to articulate what it needs to do to be successful, it is very difficult for IT to draw alongside in this conversation and deliver meaningful change.
☐	14.1.3 What is the perception of the IT function within the business?	The business volume drills into this topic in more detail but the key here is that if IT is relegated to the role of keeping the lights on, it will take some effort to win hearts and minds and elevate the role of IT to that of trusted advisor to the business.
☐	14.1.4 Has the business undertaken an exercise to align IT strategy with the business strategy?	This is where real traction starts to take place. The objective here is to map business objectives to IT objectives to make sure that the IT function is delivering the capability to the business in the way and at the pace they need to consume it to be successful.

☒	Question	Why this matters
☐	14.1.5 Can the business clearly articulate what IT delivery and transformation programmes are aligned to what specific business goal and how the delivered IT capability will specifically contribute to the stated goal?	If the business has a strategy and the IT group has a strategy and they are both aligned, you are in a good place to deliver on the vision. You may, however, still have a need to ensure the business stakeholders understand this plan and have bought in to its importance. The fact the plans exists is good. Everyone having them front of mind and actively using and adjusting them over time is much better.
☐	14.1.6 If the answers to questions 16.1.4 and .5 are no, would the business be prepared to engage on a body of work to understand and document these objectives?	If none of this exists in your organisation, then it is important to get some commitment to undertake some of this planning work. This is something you can do internally, or alternatively there are external consultancies which can help with this important piece of work.
☐	14.1.7 Do senior IT stakeholders in the business see their role as a key contributor to the overall business success?	Unless and until IT leaders accept their importance to driving home the business' strategic vision, they will remain relegated to a supporting role. If you don't have people within your IT team who accept this responsibility, get new people.

☒	Question	Why this matters
☐	14.1.8 Is the business locked in to a multi-year outsource? If so what options are there to deliver services alongside this?	Traditional outsource contracts, predominately, seek to avoid change and maintain the status quo. They are incompatible with a COM. If you are currently outsourced, understand what you can do outside of this relationship to start to gear the business up for when it's next renewed and you can insource again or engage a modern outsourcing partner.
☐	14.1.9 Does your organisation have a concept of charge back for IT services or do IT hold all the IT budgets?	One of the major benefits of moving to a cloud model is visibility into the cost of delivering IT to enable you to cross-charge other departments. If these departments have not had to pay for their IT before, they may not see this as a positive step!
☐	14.1.10 Do you have a specific vision to deliver a multi-cloud strategy?	Multi-cloud sounds great. Why wouldn't you want it? In reality, it's orders of magnitude more complex than you might realise and doesn't necessarily deliver any huge benefits. It's a decision not to take likely.
☐	14.1.11 What is driving your decision to go multi-cloud?	If you do want to go multi-cloud, what is the driving factor behind this decision? Is it cost optimisation? Avoiding lock-in? Leveraging capabilities unique to a specific cloud platform? There are, occasionally, valid reasons. If you really want to go multi-cloud make sure you clearly and concisely explain the reasons why you want to do this. You'll need it later when you have to justify the huge additional complexity.
☐	14.1.12 If you do want to go multi-cloud can you hedge the complexity risk?	There are strategies that allow you to hedge against the additional risk and complexity, such as choosing a development platform consistent across all. Container platforms such as Kubernetes can help.

☒	Question	Why this matters
☐	14.1.13 If you do want to go multi-cloud can you leverage common tooling?	Along with deployment, monitoring and management is equally important in a multi-cloud world. Choose a solution, such as Azure Log Analytics, which works across different clouds.
☐	14.1.14 Do you have legacy applications which might not move to the public cloud?	There are a number of reasons why your applications might not move to the public cloud. They might have physical hardware dependencies (such as dongles). They might run on legacy hardware (such as mainframes or specialist machines). You might not be able to licence your applications within a virtualised world. In these situations, you need to consider a hybrid cloud strategy.
☐	14.1.15 Have you just made significant investments into replacement hardware?	There are reasons why organisations might have done this. Your hardware might have been so elderly and so unreliable that you just had no choice. You might have been led to believe that a private cloud was the same as a public cloud. You might not have discovered cloud early enough. Whilst having done this can lead to challenges in adopting public cloud, in a hybrid world you might still be able to take advantages of some public cloud capabilities.
☐	14.1.16 Do you have differing data storage / security requirements?	Many organisations, especially public sector ones, have specific rules on what data can be stored where. Whilst official and official sensitive data can be stored in the public cloud, secret can't. In this circumstance, hybrid can deliver some major advantages, allowing you to construct a COM which straddles public and on premises cloud, whilst delivering dedicated hardware within a traditional datacentre for high-security requirements. Appliances such as Azure Stack can help here.

☒	Question	Why this matters
☐	14.1.17 Do you have a need to store large quantities of historical data?	Hybrid can play an important role here, allowing frequently accessed, "hot" data, to remain on premises, while historical, infrequently accessed data can be moved to the public cloud.
☐	14.1.18 Do you need a quick to implement disaster recovery solution?	Hybrid can also play an important role here, with your primary environment remaining on premises, but your fail-over, disaster recovery environment moving to the public cloud.
☐	14.1.19 Do you run VMWare on premises today?	Whilst VMWare was the gold standard in days gone by, it has failed to keep up with the industry's move to public cloud. Its aborted attempt to get into this world with vCloud Air was mothballed. If you run VMWare on premises today, you will struggle to fully realise a hybrid cloud world. Having said that, VMWare on Azure is soon to be released which will at least offer some hybrid capabilities.
☐	14.1.20 Are you a Global organisation with both centralised and regional deployments of workloads?	You will need to spend some time working through your network connectivity plans before you start deploying workloads. You may end up with multiple Hybrid data centres in region with international back haul over your own infrastructure. Microsoft has ExpressRoute premium which will allow you to use some of their international bandwidth to join Azure regions which you need to consider in your overall network design.

14.2 Procurement and Financial Governance

Once you've decided upon your cloud strategy, you need to build processes around procuring it and governing it.

The way you procure cloud services will be very different from the way you might have procured on premises software. The organisations you procure it from will likely change. The questions you ask of providers will almost certainly change.

Dealing with how you allocate and manage the cost associated with your new cloud environment will also fundamentally change. These charges will move from fixed up-front costs to variable on-going costs. You will have the capability to spend *more* than your thought you would but also the opportunity, with work and attention, to spend *less* than you thought. These challenges and opportunities need to be understood and managed.

☒	Question	Why this matters
☐	14.2.1 How does your business account for IT spend at the moment?	You may already have a sophisticated mechanism for understanding IT cost today, based on cost per user numbers and cost per line of business application. Alternatively, you may have a few big lines in your P&L and a lack of structure behind this.
☐	14.2.2 Can you state your IT costs per user or per application?	If you can't do this today, start to think about how you might represent this in your procurement and IT accounting costs. These will start to be the pillars you build on moving forwards.
☐	14.2.3 Do you normally wait until year end to bag the best deal from vendors?	Whilst the quarter end and year end pattern will never completely disappear from vendors, with a consumption-based model and an inability for the vendor to book revenue in line with orders, steep discounts to plug a gap in their numbers don't typically exist within a cloud world.
☐	14.2.4 Where do you buy your IT licences and services from today?	Historically, most IT licence spend was with IT resellers or Licence Service Providers (LSPs). In this new world, licences can now be procured from a number of different people and styles of organisations. Cloud managed services businesses (MSPs) can bundles professional services and cloud consumption into one bill.
☐	14.2.5 Do you expect large discounts from vendors?	Whilst there are still some discounts associated with large commitments, typically for SaaS solutions, with IaaS and PaaS platforms, the margins are substantially lower and there is less opportunity for the vendor to offer these discounts. Instead, often vendors will leverage investment funds to pay for workloads to be moved to the cloud to drive increased usage and consumption.

☒	Question	Why this matters
☐	14.2.6 Have you chosen Microsoft as one of your strategic cloud partners?	Your procurement pipeline is an important asset to allow you to work with multiple cloud providers, you will typically have a different process to engage with your strategic partners. If you've already chosen Microsoft, don't let setting up a procurement pipeline for other vendors stop you getting to work with your strategic partners.
☐	14.2.7 Do you have a set of procurement questions that are fit for a cloud world?	Many traditional RFP sets of questions don't fit in this new world. You'll need to review them and work towards a new set that are fit for purpose. We have included a sample of the kinds of questions you might ask below.
☐	14.2.8 Where is your SaaS application delivered from?	Many SaaS vendors use a cloud deployment model themselves. If they use one of the major cloud providers, ideally one you use yourselves, you can forgo many of the detailed hosting questions you may have asked in the past as you will already know the answers to them.
☐	14.2.9 Do you use an IaaS or PaaS deployment model?	There is no right or wrong answer to this, but typically an IaaS deployment model may suggest a legacy application which has been "cloud washed". Vendors using PaaS will have needed to have done extensive rearchitecting which demonstrates their real commitment to cloud.
☐	14.2.10 What is your shared responsibility model with your cloud provider?	Firstly, they should immediately understand this question. If they don't panic. Cloud vendors support SaaS vendors to some extent, depending on whether it's IaaS or PaaS. SaaS vendors should know intimately what they are responsible for and what the cloud vendor is responsible for and should have a documented RACI matrix for this.

☒	Question	Why this matters
☐	14.2.11 What is your high availability/ disaster recovery (HA/DR) plan?	A cloud deployment model doesn't magically give SaaS providers HA/DR out of the box. These concepts are as important in a cloud deployment model as an on premises one. Make sure your SaaS vendor has thought through all these challenges and has a good answer to them.
☐	14.2.12 What is your SLA?	When you move to a SaaS-based application you are going to be wholly reliant on the SLA of your SaaS provider. How does their SLA intersect with that of their hosting provider? Have they carefully thought through composite SLAs based on the range of cloud services their application hosting leverages?
☐	14.2.13 What technology stack do you use? What is your architecture?	Whilst less important due to the nature of SaaS delivery it's always interesting to know what technologies the SaaS provider uses. Do they use a traditional relational database or a schema-less NOSQL database? Do they use SOAP or REST service endpoints? All of these will give you clues about how serious and technically sophisticated the vendor is.
☐	14.2.14 Is your solution single tenanted or multi-tenanted?	Again, there is no right or wrong answer to this. Vendors might choose single-tenancy for compliance or performance reasons, alternatively they might choose it because they don't want to invest the time to rearchitect for the cloud. Typically, a multi-tenanted design is better as it reduces the vendor's cost, which they can pass on to you, and it demonstrates it is actually SaaS software, not just on premises software "delivered through the cloud".

☒	Question	Why this matters
☐	14.2.15 What is your update frequency?	True SaaS vendors will operate on an "ever green" basis and make frequent changes to their code base. Those that only deliver updates every few months probably haven't fully embraced cloud / DevOps within their own organisation.
☐	14.2.16 Does all IT spend need to go through procurement?	Traditionally, when there were large CAPEX spends behind infrastructure projects, this approach made sense. With smaller procurements from cloud vendors, this model can become prohibitively time consuming and expensive.
☐	14.2.17 How are IT budgets expressed and spent today?	With cloud deployment models, configuration changes or adding and removing users can have substantial and immediate effect on your usage charges. Budgets need to become much more flexible and capable of being "spent" without as much control and governance as you may have today. Techniques such as quotas rather than budgets can make more sense.
☐	14.2.18 Do you have the ability to apply budgets to departments or cost centres?	Much of the governance you will introduce to your cloud environment will be the enforcing of cost allocation. In order to enforce this allocation, you need to have the appropriate level of granularity within your existing cost code structure.
☐	14.2.19 Do you have approach levels of delegation within your budget and cost code structure?	By using cloud, you have fine grained control of who, at what level, can spend what. This is something you may consider within your budgeting and financial governance model. For example, a person in role x can increase spend by up to £x / hour, but someone lower down in the organisation in position y can only increase costs by £y / hour. This allows a shift from an absolute to a relative definition of a budget.

☒	Question	Why this matters
☐	14.2.20 Who is now in charge of monitoring spend and introducing optimisation?	No matter how hard you try and what controls you put in place, you will almost certainly end up spending more than you should. There will be things left on or licences connected to people that don't need them. There will be servers deployed that are too big or not being used. There may be defects which drive increased consumption. As you move to the cloud, place someone in charge of cost optimisation. Someone whose entire job revolves around asking all the annoying questions about why this is needed and why the specification of a given server is too high. Give them tools to help them do this programmatically and automatically.

14.3 Service Management

Service management is at the core of your existing IT operating model. It governs just about everything related to how you consume and manage your IT services.

Whilst you almost certainly have a fairly slick process today, your service management realm will likely need extensive attention and change as you move into a Cloud Operating Model.

ITIL has served us all well over the years, but some of the prescriptive processes in its current version may not be your bedrock into the future.

☒	Question	Why this matters
☐	14.3.1 Do you use ITIL today?	ITIL offers a lot of value to organisations today and will likely evolve to consider the rise of cloud and agility, but in its current form, it can introduce additional complexity and processes which can severely impact on the effective rollout of your COM.
☐	14.3.2 Do you use SIAM today?	Service Integration and Management (SIAM) was a great product of its time. It allowed large, monolithic and complex IT operating environments to be broken up into "bite-sized" chunks and distributed to different service organisations. The idea behind it is still valid, its current implementation is not hugely appropriate for a next generation COM.
☐	14.3.3 Are you locked in to a SIAM model?	You may well have contracted with a SIAM provider, or have SIAM constructs embedded within your existing operating model. If you do, it doesn't mean you can't introduce a COM, but if you do, you will almost certainly have to free it from the bounds and controls that your other towers need to adhere to.
☐	14.3.4 Do you want to bring in additional partners into a multi-source model?	For organisations that have been completely outsourced, bringing additional partners in can be challenging. Consider how you will manage these additional partners alongside your incumbent. You may need to introduce a role or team responsible for vendor management and integration.
☐	14.3.5 How will you manage integration between these partners?	Whenever you have multiple partners or vendors there are additional complexities around how these partners and vendors will work together. Ensure you spend the time to fully map out the interdependencies and the processes you will use to hand off between these people in a controlled way.

☒	Question	Why this matters
☐	14.3.6 Are you able to break your IT service provision into a portfolio approach?	Portfolio is the more modern approach to IT service delivery. Rather than individual service lines, think about how these can be grouped-up into cross-tower functional capabilities which can be presented back into the business.
☐	14.3.7 Do you have a mature incident management process?	Great. You typically won't need to make major changes to this. Incidents will still occur in the cloud. You'll need to manage them. Some will be minor, some will be major. Understand how you will interface and get updates from the new players in your process, but for the most part we're talking evolution not revolution.
☐	14.3.8 Can you automate any of your incident management processes?	With a move to the cloud there are increasing opportunities to automate things and incident management is a ripe candidate. Can you automatically undertake remediation work to fix a known problem? Can you apply AI and machine learning to automatically make suggestions to support operators on things that they can try?
☐	14.3.9 Can you apply a blow it away and recreate it rather than fix it mindset?	With increasing automation and standardisation, there will be less and less need to actually "fix" things. In the same way you thrown away a broken TV today and just buy a new one, your IT environment will be similar in the future. If a laptop is misbehaving, factory reset it and automatically rebuild it rather than trying to fix the problem. The same can be true for servers and application environments.

☒	Question	Why this matters
☐	14.3.10 How mature is your change management process?	Change management will be the most profoundly impacted by a move to the cloud. Change management in the front line in the battle between agility and control. It is purposely designed to "reduce risk" which in turn means resisting change. Map out your change process and understand how you need to go about changing it (no pun intended).
☐	14.3.11 Do you require all changes to go to a change advisory board (CAB)	CABs generally serve two purposes. Firstly, to inform everyone about what is happening and secondly to allow people to speak up if they identify risk as part of a change. The first can now be achieved by other means, such as Teams and the second should become less and less of an issue as change becomes the norm rather than the exception. Review what changes *really* need to go to a CAB and which can bypass it moving forwards with appropriate controls and guard rails in place.
☐	14.3.12 How will you deal with lighting up new capabilities on the platform?	The evergreen nature of cloud services means new features will appear continuously. You need to understand how you will deal with this and release these new capabilities to users.
☐	14.3.13 Do you have early adopters / champions internally?	One approach to this constant change is to nominate a cross section of your user population to act as a test bed for these new capabilities before being rolled out to the wider user group. In this model you can undertake proofs of concept and detailed testing.

☒	Question	Why this matters
☐	14.3.14 Do you have tiered support teams across each of your service lines?	As you move further up the cloud IaaS > PaaS > SaaS stack there will be less and less requirement for in-house second- and third-line support teams as these will be provided by the cloud vendor. Think about how you can redeploy these capabilities internally, for instance into automation teams.
☐	14.3.15 How will you interface with your cloud vendor's support organisation?	You will invariably need support fairly regularly from your cloud vendors, either in regard to service or configuration issues. You need to understand who will deliver this and how it will be delivered. Will you interface directly with the vendor? Via a reseller? Via your cloud managed services provider? Understand the roles and responsibilities in the chain and what you will need to do in the future.
☐	14.3.16 Do you have a Microsoft Premier Support Agreement?	In your COM you will need to consider which participants hold which support contracts. If you are working with a cloud managed service provider that has a Microsoft Premier contract and can make it available to you, do you need your own one moving forwards?
☐	14.3.17 How will you support internally developed applications?	As you move into a world of automation and DevOps your support organisation will profoundly change. Service impacting issues will move from being predominantly infrastructure or configuration issues to being predominantly code and automation issues. Think about how your platform services and development teams will actively play a part in the support organisation. "It worked in test" will not cut it moving forwards. Developers and automation specialists best start getting ready for that call at 3am.

☒	Question	Why this matters
☐	14.3.18 Do you have shadow IT in place today outside your control?	You may already have applications and services which sit outside your service management realm. You need to consider how you bring these into this new service management structure.
☐	14.3.19 Do you have clear and measurable business and technology SLAs in place today?	SLAs change radically as you move into this cloud world. You need to understand how you can meet your existing SLAs and manage the SLAs associated with the matrix of new suppliers and vendors that form part of your COM. You may consider introducing new measure and KPIs such as Net Promoter Score (NPS) to understand the success and operation of your new COM?
☐	14.3.20 Are you familiar with ULAs and VLAs	User Level Agreements (ULAs) and Value Level Agreements (VLAs) are the direction of travel for the interface between business and IT. You need to understand them as concepts and build a path to how you can deliver against these new metrics.

14.4 Access Control, Security and Provisioning

Getting access to and securing your new cloud environment is of paramount importance. Security used to the be the big blocker for moving to the cloud. More often than not, this has now been reversed and cloud vendors lead with the security of their offerings. Many still haven't quite made that leap.

Using a secure cloud platform is only half the solution. It's no point having a state-of-the-art security on your house or car if you leave it unlocked. Security in the cloud is a shared model. The vendor is responsible for a great deal. You'll be responsible for a fair bit.

You'll need to think about this challenge through multiple lenses. You'll need to think about identity and access control. You'll need to think about physical and network security. Finally, you'll need to think about how you provide these capabilities to users and make sure your provisioning and JML processes are secure.

☒	Question	Why this matters
☐	14.4.1 Do you have a Chief Information Security Officer?	If you do, get them involved right now. Put the book down. Send them an email. Tell them you want to meet as soon as possible to get them onboard with what you are thinking. If you don't, you'll regret it down the line. They can be your greatest ally or fiercest challenge. Find out which they will be as soon as you can.
☐	14.4.2 What is your CISO's approach to risk?	CISOs come from a range of different backgrounds and many have a fundamentally different approach to risk. Some will be open minded. Some will be set in their ways. If they love to see low level infrastructure designs you're going to need to help them see beyond these. The quicker you can identify how supportive they will be with your cloud journey, the sooner you can find out how much time you need to set aside to get them on board. Without them, you're dead in the water.
☐	14.4.3 Does your organisation have a documented set of security principles and rules?	If you do, this may be a good thing, or it may be a bad thing. If it runs to hundreds of pages you're in for a lot of work, but at least you have a strong framework to build to. Get hold of it, read it, get a sense of how specific (i.e. related to traditional methods and models) it is, or whether it just describes high level principles and rules. If it simply describes best practices, you're good to go as you can easily replicate these within a cloud context. If they mandate things like VPNs and physical access tokens you're going to need to get them changed, fast.
☐	14.4.4 Do you use Active Directory on premises today?	Your cloud identity model, typically, is built directly from your on premises Active Directory environment.

☒	Question	Why this matters
☐	14.4.5 What state in your Active Directory in today?	Moving to a cloud identity model means your on premises environment has to be in good shape. Things that you might have gotten away with on premises, such as duplicate namespaces and accounts including rogue characters, just won't cut the mustard in the cloud. You may have acquired other organisations and bolted their ADs onto yours. Before you do anything, get your existing environment checked over. Get a report on how it looks and what you need to do.
☐	14.4.6 Do you use physical access tokens today?	Physical access tokens were great. They served a purpose in their time. With the cloud, there are a multitude of newer, better, technologies to use, such as Azure MFA. These technologies are much more cost effective and allow a range of second factors of authentication, such as phone calls, text messages and mobile apps. They can even stretch to physical proximity of the phone to the laptop or geo location.
☐	14.4.7 Do you have an on premises single sign-on solution in place?	You may leverage Active Directory Federation Services (ADFS) today to provide single sign-on to users. If you do, you will probably have a number of connections you set up manually, exchanging certificates and keys. It probably works OK most of the time. You can probably keep this in place, for some things, but you'll also probably want to migrate it to something a bit more up-to-date.

☒	Question	Why this matters
☐	14.4.8 Do you have a cloud-based single sign-on solution?	There are a number of cloud-based single sign-on solutions in market. Okta is one of the best known. These solutions do a great job and you will already be experiencing many of the benefits of moving to a new cloud IdP. If you do have these solutions in place, understand the capabilities available natively on Azure, such as Azure Active Directory to see whether you still need these third-party solutions moving forwards.
☐	14.4.9 How are licences impacted for JML in a cloud world?	JML in a cloud world is very different from an on premises world. Providing access and revoking access to cloud-based services starts and stops cost being accrued in near real time. It also requires licences to be available in near real time. Depending on how you buy your licences, ensure you either have sufficient head-room to support bringing users on line quickly enough if you're on an EA, or that you fully understand the mechanism to get additional licences if you are on CSP.
☐	14.4.10 How does security change for JML in a cloud world?	Whilst single sign-on is great, it also means users have access to a great deal of data and different services, wherever they are. You need to ensure that your JML process is quick enough to switch off access to these third-party systems in line with employees moving roles or leaving the organisation.
☐	14.4.11 What security solution do you use on premises?	You probably use of the big brand security solutions on premises today, such as Check Point, F5, Barracuda etc. Understand what that vendor's story around public cloud is. Do they support it? What is their licencing and deployment model?

☒	Question	Why this matters
☐	14.4.12 Do you require dedicated connectivity to your on premises environment?	The answer to this is almost certainly yes, so you need to understand what options you have available from your current telecoms provider. Do they support ExpressRoute? Which flavour? Who supports what?
☐	14.4.13 Do you want to route all your cloud traffic, including internet breakout, on premises?	The immediate answer to this is often yes, and yes is sometimes ok, but understand the implications of this from a cost and performance perspective. Does *everything* have to transit via this route or can you separate out some traffic, such as Microsoft Updates?
☐	14.4.14 Do you need to inspect and control the ingress and egress of traffic to the cloud?	Azure and ExpressRoute have very sophisticated controls round data routing, and access control, but limited capabilities around traffic inspection. You may need to consider additional security products and services to fully inspect this traffic.
☐	14.4.15 What are your policies today on internal network security?	There are many approaches today to segregating traffic within internal networks, including VLANs. Understand how these map to the cloud. Moving to the cloud can also be a good excuse to ramp up your internal network security controls as they manifest within the cloud. It's much simpler now to enforce stricter access control rules between network segments or require additional controls such as IPSEC.
☐	14.4.16 Do you use host-based firewalls and other controls?	If you don't use these on premises today, explore whether you can introduce them as part of your move to the cloud. Best practice now is to have as much security within your networks as between and into your networks.
☐	14.4.17 Do you employ a service catalogue today?	Carefully consider how a traditional service catalogue fits into your new COM. Whilst a service catalogue can be useful for some aspects of provisioning, in other ways it can be constricting.

☒	Question	Why this matters
☐	14.4.18 Can you embrace the notion of cloud environments?	A cloud environment can be a more useful construct to dovetail into a service catalogue. This can allow users to self-service provision through your own service portal, but still use the native capabilities, such as the Azure Portal and APIs, to provision individual capabilities and services.
☐	14.4.19 What information would you need to collect from your users at the point of provisioning a cloud environment?	There is a lot of information you *could* collect from users as part of a provisioning process. Try to balance the need for comprehensive reporting with making the process as easy and stream-lined as possible.
☐	14.4.20 Do you have a requirement to span policy across multiple clouds or provide additional reporting on compliance?	Azure Policy is specific to Azure. It is also policed by Azure. Some organisations may want to enforce policies across multiple clouds or they might want to provide a separate, independent view of their compliance. Third party tools can provide additional capabilities in this space. Examples include: Palo Alto Evident, NeuVector and DivvyCloud.

14.5 Monitoring, Management and Automation

Monitoring, management and automation are at the heart of your COM. In this chapter we specifically focussed on managing your estate, as it looks today, in the cloud. Azure provides a range of capabilities which can assist in terms of automating your heritage workloads as you go through a journey to make them more cloud-native.

In the chapter we describe this model as a Gartner mode 1.5 – somewhere in between a legacy, on premises environment and a brand new, cloud native, mode 2.

Moving to a more modern approach to monitoring and managing heritage workloads can have a profound impact on your ITOM and will almost certainly involve migrating to cloud-native tooling which can be a major undertaking.

In these questions we'll hopefully help you to start to understand this first stage of your journey to being cloud-native.

☒	Question	Why this matters
☐	14.5.1 What tool do you use for monitoring and managing your environment today?	There will probably only be a handful of people expert on your monitoring and management "operating model". It's probably something that's been there for ever and just sits in the background doing its thing. Find out who's your expert and do some research.
☐	14.5.2 Do you have one, or a number of different tools?	You may have tried migrating tools in the past. You may have a mix of different tools, doing different things, from different vendors. Your tool for monitoring patches may be different from your tool for monitoring desktops. Understand the entire landscape of your toolchain and ideally draw it up into a diagram, if you don't have one already.
☐	14.5.3 Do you use System Center?	If you do, great. Your job will be easier. If you don't it's not a massive problem, you will probably need to migrate to new tooling anyways. You may just have a bit more work to do.
☐	14.5.4 Is your current monitoring system designed for an on premises world?	Many of the tools in market today (including System Center) were built in the days of on premises. The clue is in the name of some of them, such as *Lan*Guard. These tools naturally continue to evolve and support more cloud workloads, but it's often very difficult to use these tools to support your new cloud-native monitoring and management operating model.
☐	14.5.5 What tool do you use for backup today?	In the same way that monitoring and management tools were designed for the on premises world, so too were backup solutions. You need to consider whether this solution is still valid in a cloud world, or whether you can leverage cloud-native tooling. You may be able to utilise a hybrid, where your existing solution hands off long-term storage to the cloud.

☒	Question	Why this matters
☐	14.5.6 How do you do server patching today?	In a server world, the process is largely similar, but you now have the ability to make greater use of automation to power the end-to-end patch cycle across complex architectures. Azure can also automatically patch IaaS machines if you enable this
☐	14.5.7 How do you do device patching today?	In the devices world, with modern management, typically clients now take their updates directly from Microsoft, governed by Intune. Typically, users have these updates forced on to them as part of the evergreen Windows as a Service.
☐	14.5.8 Are your devices primarily on site or remote?	With modern device management, devices become cloud-enrolled rather than on premises. This can have advantages (better support for remote working) and disadvantages (additional complexity managing large number of office-based devices). Carefully plan your hybrid device management solution.
☐	14.5.9 How complex is your AD GPO structure?	In this new world of modern device management, Intune and MDM replaces Active Directory and GPOs. Depending on the complexity of the policies you enforce today, there could be substantial work involved in migrating to policies to MDM.
☐	14.5.10 What edition of Windows 10 do you use today?	Many of the advanced, modern management, capabilities are only available in Enterprise. You may need to reconsider your licencing strategy for devices. Enterprise is now available under the CSP licencing program (it was just EA).
☐	14.5.11 Do you use gold images to deploy OSes to devices?	With modern management, gold images are typically no longer required. Devices connect straight to Azure AD from the OOTB experience and immediately come under device control, are hardened and have applications deployed to them.

☒	Question	Why this matters
☐	14.5.12 How comfortable are you with cloud domain-joining your devices?	With a move away from traditional Active Directory to Azure Active, management and security of those devices is now delivered exclusively from the cloud.
☐	14.5.13 Are you aware of the release and support cadence for Windows 10?	There are two versions of Windows 10, semi-annual and long-term service branch. Microsoft are encouraging users on to the semi-annual branch. The support model has recently changed, whereby the September release will have support for 30 months and the March release will have support for 18 months. Consider how you will deal with this rapid update cycle for the underlying operating system.
☐	14.5.14 How do you install applications on devices today?	Automatic deployment of software installation packages via GPO and/or platforms like System Center Configuration Manager (SCCM) is common-place. With modern management, these packages are deployed from the cloud. You need to consider the amount of work involved in changing your application deployment methodology.
☐	14.5.15 What anti-virus software do you use today?	Most of the AV providers have embraced a cloud world and their solutions play nicely with the cloud. Others don't. The capabilities of Windows Defender have also evolved substantially over the past few years, which may negate the need for third party solutions.

☒	Question	Why this matters
☐	14.5.16 To what extent do you envisage substantial portions of your server infrastructure remaining on premises?	This is an important design point and has substantial implications for how you design your monitoring and management solution. If the majority of the world will live in the cloud in the near future, solely using cloud-native technology (such as Azure Log Analytics) may be appropriate. If lots of on premises equipment will remain, you may need to keep System Center or equivalent alongside it, at least for now.
☐	14.5.17 How much automation do you do today?	There are a lot of things you can automate on premises, especially when combined with virtualisation technologies. If you're doing this today, great. You'll just be doing a whole heap more of it in the cloud and will have the ability to do things that you can't do on premises today.
☐	14.5.18 What is your team's level of skill with PowerShell?	PowerShell is the scripting language of choice within the Microsoft cloud. If your team are not already whizzes on it, they need to become whizzes. Fast. Consider how you can support your team to upskill on this technology.
☐	14.5.19 How do you respond to alerts today?	Alert management is difficult. How do you filter the noise of warnings and spot the actual critical incident you need to fix? This is one area where the cloud can assist with machine learning, spotting the trends and finding that needle in the haystack.
☐	14.5.20 To what extent can you take corrective actions in relation to an alert?	If there are things you commonly have to do to fix an application that is malfunctioning, such as forcing a config update, can you automate this? Tools such as Azure Automation can be programmed with complex logic about what to do in different situations and what to do to fix a problem.

14.6 DevOps and Application Development

Successfully restructuring your organisation to take advantage of DevOps is one of the most challenging aspects of fully embracing a Cloud Operating Model.

It will have the biggest impact on your organisational structure of any of the changes you need to make. It will also be the set of changes which helps you best deliver and execute your COM.

If every business needs to become a software business, then every business really needs to build a DevOps culture and team within their organisation.

☒	Question	Why this matters
☐	14.6.1 Do you have an internal development function?	If you don't currently develop software today, this can be an advantage as you won't have an existing team to morph.
☐	14.6.2 Do you want an internal development function?	If the answer to the previous question was no, this question is of paramount importance. Getting into software development is not to be done lightly, but in order to really digitally differentiate yourself, it's increasingly necessary.
☐	14.6.3 Do you have a software development lifecycle management (SDLC) tool in place?	Most organisations that do development today, will have an existing SDLC in place. You might use Team Foundation Server. You might use the Atlassian stack. You will need to make extensive use of this SDLC tool as part of your DevOps initiative. Make sure you have one that properly supports it.
☐	14.6.4 Do you have a preference on software development language and frameworks?	There is no right answer to this question. With Microsoft's cloud there is no preference for one language or framework over another. .NET is the typical framework used by "Microsoft Shops" but it doesn't need to be. Java, Node, Go, Ruby and any other framework work seamlessly. If you have no preference look to the availability and cost of resources to determine the best choice for you.
☐	14.6.5 Do you have an established operations team supporting your developers?	If you do, you may need to fundamentally rethink how they work alongside your developers. The role of the operations team will need to change. Start by evaluating their skillsets and understanding their level of competency in scripting and automation.
☐	14.6.6 Do your development and operations reporting lines converge?	It's vital that development and operations report, ultimately, to the same person. It's the only way to truly embrace DevOps. If they don't, collapse the teams and put one leader in charge of both teams.

☒	Question	Why this matters
☐	14.6.7 Can you sustain rapid code releases?	Along with changes to roles, the biggest change in adopting DevOps is enabling rapid change. You need to understand if your codebase can support this.
☐	14.6.8 Do you have a modular architecture?	Further to rapid change, if your current application(s) have a monolithic architecture, enabling rapid and frequent deployments may cause problems.
☐	14.6.9 Do you have centralised configuration management?	The vast majority of software defects trace back to configuration management issues. If you don't have centralised configuration management, you need it.
☐	14.6.10 How do you manage environments today?	In a world of DevOps, the traditional notion of environments fades away. With ephemeral environments, you can have as many or as few environments as you want. Consider how many environments you need and how you can support these.
☐	14.6.11 Do you utilise third party components or libraries?	In a world of automated deployment, you need to consider how easy it is to bundle and deploy third party libraries. You also need to understand any licencing implications of having more environments than you might have used previously.
☐	14.6.12 Is your application based on third party platforms?	If your application is hosted inside another platform (such as SharePoint or Sitecore) you will need to do extensive research on how to support automated deployment in this model.
☐	14.6.13 Have you investigated containers?	Containers are the cool kids on the block right now. There can be significant benefits of containerisation, but there are also some drawbacks and additional platforms you need to orchestrate these containers.
☐	14.6.14 Can you leverage platform services?	Wherever possible, look to leverage PaaS components as part of your application architecture to make deployments easier and maintenance more straightforward.

☒	Question	Why this matters
☐	14.6.15 What delivery platform do you want to use?	There are a multitude of models to build and deploy code today. You might choose PaaS, containers, functions or something else. Make the choice carefully as it will have a profound impact.
☐	14.6.16 To what extent are you prepared to accept "lock-in"?	It's easy to say you are not in any way prepared to accept "lock-in". Understand the ramifications of this statement. Some lock-in is sometimes ok to reduce development effort or if you perceive the cost of reversing out of an environment to be less than the cost of making it work within a different cloud in the future.
☐	14.6.17 Do you have availability requirements beyond that supplied by Azure?	Most applications can function within the SLAs offered by Microsoft, as long as the correct design patterns are adhered to and you utilise multiple datacentres. Some applications simply can't ever go down and in this circumstance, you might want to investigate hosting across different cloud providers.
☐	14.6.18 What is your approach to testing?	One of the major prerequisites to embracing DevOps is automated testing. It's the safety net that allows rapid deployments. If you don't currently have unit tests, you need to investigate the feasibility of introducing them.
☐	14.6.19 Can you automate your UI testing?	Testing code is great. To really rest safe in the knowledge changes are not breaking things, you must implement UI testing.
☐	14.6.20 Can you automate integration testing?	Along with testing the UI, also consider how you can automate the end-to-end testing of your solution in place. You may need mocked end points to help with this.

Chapter

Funny you should say that

Laughter gives us distance. It allows us to step back from an event, deal with it and then move on.

Bob Newhart (Comedian, 1929 –)

F OR many organisations the availability of a credible cloud operating model cannot come soon enough. It is the missing piece for organisations with increasing (and in some cases total) reliance on cloud services and the need to develop an organisational culture that has the business teams and IT team working in harmony. It will also help those organisations that have dipped their toes in the cloud and then thought; what are we getting into? If you have yet to start your journey in the cloud then; what have you been waiting for?

You will have noticed on the book cover the yellow sticky with three words:

Secure: we tell you all the capabilities to switch on to secure your environment

Compliant: so your IT environment meets your governance and policy requirements (e.g. data encryption, data residency)

Agile: and this is the crux of the book about how you deliver *agility* to the business team and *control* for the IT team who has day-to-day responsibility for this strategic resource.

The best person to ask experience of is someone who has climbed the mountain rather than someone who looked at the pictures and thought, one day, maybe. Now we have the experience shared by those that chose to climb the mountain rather than look at the pictures.

If you have your own story, then we encourage you to share it at stories@smart-questions.com

John Kendrick

Cloud Transformation Lead, International Oil Company

Moving to "cloud" was (and I should say still is) an emotional and challenging journey. The classic PPT (People Process Tools) activity goes into overdrive... Do not underestimate the impact, effort and how long this will take! That said, the benefits are huge.

Classic infrastructure generally takes weeks or months to setup kit in data centres with many teams involved. It's expensive and slow... and often processes used have been in place for many, many years.

The cloud proposition is significantly better ... but the disruption it brings is significant too! Creating vanilla infrastructure in the Cloud takes tens of minutes, but, all the hardening processes, port opening, active directory setup, everything that exist around it is from a time when infrastructure took weeks and months to get setup, and generally geared to have an SLAs (Service Level Agreements) that is setup to respond within in days (if not weeks); the SLAs are just not ready, and because of this, nor are the people.

When I embarked on it, we didn't realise quite how much disruption we would cause. We spent a long time doing what we could to automate as much as we could within our new processes. Automation of process within your own control should be non-negotiable – anything that involves your new cloud platform must be automated as much as possible – remember, this is Infrastructure as Code, so treat it like that. However, no matter how fast you go, no matter how much automation you bring through your new cloud construct, you can't get away from the fact that there are significant changes needed to "external" teams and processes. Assuming your company follows it, ITIL v3 will need to be interpreted in a very different light to ensure its alignment to the speed of cloud.

Even when you battle through and as you begin to change the people, process and technology, you encounter the next challenge –

the operating model. There are two elements to this. One, having a customer focus is really core – you need to create a service people want to use. Amazon and Microsoft have different technology offers, but they do have a very common theme of making it something that the customer wants and desires. The second is ensuring you are ready to have a service that can keep pace with the new cloud offer – and very importantly be able to "resell" it within your organisation. When we started on the Cloud journey Microsoft were just introducing ARM (moving away from Classic) and Amazon were churning out pretty significant improvements on their core products on a daily basis. We had to create an operating model that could leverage these new features, and to do this we developed a "product" based model, rather than a "project" based model to support the Cloud offers. The most significant challenge in this area was the release schedule – we were releasing improvements to enterprise cloud infrastructure every two weeks, this was across both Amazon and Azure. A lot of people saw this as a huge risk – but it was actually essential… in fact, if we didn't keep pace, there was a higher risk if we stayed on older version of the various product offers.

Cloud offers amazing capabilities and with it HUGE (and I really do mean big) positive disruption. This isn't throwing a pebble into a pond and watching the ripples move out. This is almost akin to throwing a boulder so large in that it dislodges all of the water! Metaphorically the new ways of working are the water in which you will refill.

It's a brilliant move. One I fully advocate, and, had I known what I know now back when I embarked on the journey all those months ago I probably would have been more nervous about my chance of success. That said, I don't think I would have changed anything with my approach – "do something, learn, do again, learn again, etc". It was tough, it was hard work, but I was successful, and cloud can (and if done properly will) be a positive impact on your company.

Pete Gatt

CEO, Vibrato

I'd like the share a story from one of our customers, a large ISV in Melbourne and Sydney with $Bs in transactions per year.

Cost can be a common trigger for a large organisation to move to the cloud. PAYG models are very attractive but they are often over simplified. This organisation quickly realised that the journey was a little larger than just "moving to the cloud" and "lifting and shifting". There was much more untapped and unrealised value in a move to cloud and change in operating models.

The development and QA teams were crying out for more environments and due to costs and lead times, this just wasn't happening. The cost pressures resulted in "shared" environments being long lived which led to numerous costly bugs and data issues. Additionally, there was external customer pressure on security requirements and the cost to achieve this on premises was just not palatable. What's worse… the teams involved in supporting what felt like a sinking model were growing and the stress and decline in job satisfaction was vastly rising. What was needed was a change to the overall operating model to support it. What was needed was dynamic environments which meant lots of investment in automation

Unfortunately, not all teams could be involved Day 1. BAU (Business as Usual) is a real thing and thinking that a company can just stop doing BAU and start doing cloud and DevOps is just wrong. That may work in a start-up or a green field company, but it doesn't work in an established organisation. A small set of product owners, BAs, devs, QAs, infrastructure and operational staff came together to create a "centre of excellence" with the deliberate mandate that the team would disband on completion of the first migration. Through that, the "B team" was established. Everything they did they documented. Infrastructure they coded, automation they achieved and everything they learned was shared to their own team members back in BAU team A. Interestingly, team B decided to rotate various members in and out of team A so as to ensure a community of practice existed. This occurred as they realised that the DevOps and automation practices and principals could be leveraged outside of the cloud environment constructs that they were working with.

But how did they actually move and what went first? Team B was given the most representative, but achievable product to migrate to the cloud. 2 of the 3 products within the ISV had complications that included compliance and customer comms which would have prohibited the ability to complete and therefor demonstrate value to the board in a timely fashion. The chosen product had some complexity of course, but this helped determine the strategy for migrating the greater complexity when the other 2 products came to be migrated.

Chef and other cloud-based services were selected to automate the cloud environment creation, the application container setup, the application deployment and the configuration. This delivered end to end automation. Whilst the tooling was important, it was the team and processes that mattered more. Another huge complexity that the organisation needed to be addressed was the database automation. This required more process and people thought then technology capability and conquering this helped glue the community of practice together.

Completing the first migration ensured that 80% of the environment tooling, services and developed practises and IP could be re-used, which was critical to the essence of the community of practice. Interestingly again, cost reductions weren't immediately realised so there was a question about the program moving forward from the board. Luckily, team B had proved many more tangible gains that far outweighed the simple desire of OPEX reduction.

In 3 short months, the community of practice was able to demonstrate that:

- Environment creation times for the selected product went from approximately 3 months, to 3 hours, which greatly reduced the requirement for infrastructure stuff doing mundane tasks and allowing developers to fail fast on ideation.
- The overall deployment time for an application went from 48 hours (manual) to 1 hour (automated)
- In the end (not immediately realised), costs went from an average $25K per environment month to $2.5K per environment month as there was the ability to spin up and down only when the development team required it.

- Automated testing was required for automated deployments, which enabled the company to go from 0% functional coverage to 30% coverage of critical path. This paved the way for automated testing, greatly reducing the bugs and data fixes the team needed to deal with on a daily basis.
- For the developers, an average of 2 days was returned to every single developer each week!
- Using cloud infrastructure gave the team implicit compliance sign off which enabled them to enter into new markets with clients who required this.

The biggest lesson this organisation learned was that a move to cloud could not be done successfully without a shift in culture. More importantly, it can't be achieved without executive buy in and involvement from a majority of the people within the organisation. We found that It's critically important to limit the scope and toe size being dipped into the cloud and when doing so, to restrict the impact on the BAU teams involved.

In the end… guess what, it actually wasn't cheaper when they went live in the cloud. Impressively, due to the pace of delivery and innovation that they were now afforded, the ISV was able to quickly move to subsequently reduce the costs down and achieving the reduction in OPEX that the company was looking for. Just remember, a move to cloud alongside a shift in operating model and adoption of DevOps is often a catalyst to organisational change and large organisation can be moved by the efforts of the small teams on the ground.

Chapter

16

Final Word

A conclusion is the place where you got tired of thinking.

Albert Bloch (American Artist, 1882 – 1961)

FOR the business audience; we live in interesting times. This book was inspired by conversations with Microsoft and Microsoft customers and partners that had reached a point in time in their cloud journey of no return. The evidence was for them compelling; the cloud is the future, it is where innovation lives, it rocks!

This in turn raised an important question: What does that mean for the existing IT estate and how to deal with the rapidly increasing adoption of cloud with a likely end state of being 'all in' the cloud? Some businesses are already at that point of being committed to being 'all in'. Others are starting out with unchartered waters ahead.

This book deals with the conversations that surface as a business grows its dependency on the cloud. It presents the argument for a Cloud Operating Model (Bing returns over 16M results, another reason for this book) and breaks that down into the language of the business team and IT team. The Cloud Operating Model is a discussion with the business teams and IT team as participants locking down the 'let's make this happen' rather than 'locking horns'.

Perhaps we will look back one day and ask: What was all the fuss about? For now, there is an urgent need for practicality and we hope this book serves that purpose.

F OR the Technical readers; we've covered a phenomenal amount together. We've delved deep into the business rationale behind building a COM. We've hopefully given you the business rationale behind why you might want to, and indeed need to, radically change your approach to information technology and digital within your organisation.

In the business volume, we've explored new business models. We've explored data. We've explored artificial intelligence.

We've spent some time talking about how Agile and modern project management methodologies can help you deliver value more quickly to the business and give you the agility you so crave.

In the technical book we have delivered a soup-to-nuts journey from strategizing, through buying, managing, securing, monitoring and developing using your new cloud operating model.

Your journey has just begun though.

Getting from the theory in this book to the practice inside your organisation is no mean feat. Depending on the size of your business, it might take anywhere from months to years. You potentially have decades of legacy you need to remodel and adapt. The journey will be fraught with challenges, both politically and practically. You may have to crack a few eggs. You may have to bring a few new people in and let a few people go.

This is something you will almost certainly need help with. Reach out. Speak to others that have done it before. Seek guidance, counsel and help. Get in experts who have helped other organisations and can assist in avoiding the potholes and blind alleys.

Please do not be put off though. If you can pull through and deliver your new COM, you will be setting your organisation up to succeed not only now, but for the next decade. You will deliver on a dream which has until now not been possible, combining agility and control. Putting technology at the very core of what your organisation does. Helping transform you into a truly digital business.

We finish up with just two words. **Good luck!**

Appendix - Definition of terms used in this book. Alphabetically ordered:

Artificial Intelligence

AI is highly topical and here we reference Microsoft's submitted written evidence to the House of Lords SELECT COMMITTEE ON ARTIFICIAL INTELLIGENCE.

The human-centred approach to AI that Microsoft envisions can only be realised if relevant stakeholders from industry, government, civil society and the research community collaborate on the development of shared principles to shape the use of AI technologies.

Microsoft's CEO, Satya Nadella, shared some initial thoughts on what these may be in order to start this dialogue. We believe that AI should:

1. Be designed to assist humanity;

2. Be transparent;

3. Maximise efficiencies without destroying the dignity of people;

4. Be designed for privacy;

5. Have algorithmic accountability so that humans can undo unintended harm;

6. Guard against bias.

Full report (1600 pages) at *https://www.parliament.uk/documents/lords-committees/Artificial-Intelligence/AI-Written-Evidence-Volume.pdf*

Big Data

The UK House of Commons Science and Technology Committee[36] reported on the 'Big Data Dilemma'. It is well known that we are in the midst of a data explosion and Big Data is about

---

[36] *https://publications.parliament.uk/pa/cm201516/cmselect/cmsctech/468/468.pdf*

how that data will be processed to extract its value, some say providing insights that will bring change to the way we run business and society. It also needs people who can interpret the data and therein lies a current skills shortage.

The report mentioned above makes this statement: 'even existing datasets are nowhere near fully exploited. Despite data driven companies being 10% more productive than those that do not operationalise their data, most companies estimate they are analysing just 12% of their data.'

And so, we are at the beginning of understanding the potential of Big Data and while we have the processing power the human interpretation of that data remains a challenge.

DevOps

DevOps is the union of people, process, and products to enable continuous delivery of value to our end users. The contraction of "Dev" and "Ops" refers to replacing siloed Development and Operations to create multidisciplinary teams that now work together with shared and efficient practices and tools. Essential DevOps practices include agile planning, continuous integration, continuous delivery, and monitoring of applications.

Source: *https://docs.microsoft.com/en-us/azure/devops/what-is-devops*

Infrastructure as a Service (IaaS)

The capability provided to the consumer is to provision processing, storage, networks, and other fundamental computing resources where the consumer is able to deploy and run arbitrary software, which can include operating systems and applications. The consumer does not manage or control the underlying cloud infrastructure but has control over operating systems, storage, and deployed applications; and possibly limited control of select networking components (e.g., host firewalls).

Source: *https://nvlpubs.nist.gov/*

Platform as a Service (PaaS)

The capability provided to the consumer is to deploy onto the cloud infrastructure consumer-created or acquired applications created using programming languages, libraries, services, and tools supported by the provider. The consumer does not manage or control the underlying cloud infrastructure including network, servers, operating systems, or storage, but has control over the deployed applications and possibly configuration settings for the application-hosting environment.

Source: *https://nvlpubs.nist.gov/*

Prince 2

PRINCE2 (an acronym for **PR**ojects **IN** **C**ontrolled Environments) is a de facto process-based method for effective project management. Used extensively by the UK Government, PRINCE2 is also widely recognised and used in the private sector, both in the UK and internationally. The PRINCE2 method is in the public domain and offers non-proprietorial best practice guidance on project management.

Key features of PRINCE2:

- Focus on business justification

- Defined organisation structure for the project management team

- Product-based planning approach

- Emphasis on dividing the project into manageable and controllable stages

- Flexibility that can be applied at a level appropriate to the project.

Source: *https://www.prince2.com/uk/what-is-prince2*

Robotic Process Automation (RPA)

In traditional workflow automation tools, a software developer produces a list of actions to automate a task and interface to the back-end system using internal application programming interfaces (APIs) or dedicated scripting language. In contrast, RPA systems develop the action list by watching the user perform that task in the application's graphical user interface (GUI), and then perform the automation by repeating those tasks directly in the GUI. This can lower the barrier to use of automation in products that might not otherwise feature APIs for this purpose.

Source: Wikipedia

Software as a Service (SaaS)

The capability provided to the consumer is to use the provider's applications running on a cloud infrastructure. The applications are accessible from various client devices through either a thin client interface, such as a web browser (e.g. web-based email), or a program interface. The consumer does not manage or control the underlying cloud infrastructure including network, servers, operating systems, storage, or even individual application capabilities, with the possible exception of limited user specific application configuration settings.

Source: *https://nvlpubs.nist.gov/*

Waterfall

The **waterfall model** is a relatively linear *sequential design* approach for certain areas of *engineering design*. In *software development*, it tends to be among the less iterative and flexible approaches, as progress flows in largely one direction ("downwards" like a *waterfall*) through the phases of conception, initiation, analysis, design, construction, testing, deployment and maintenance.

The waterfall development model originated in the *manufacturing* and *construction* industries; where the highly structured physical environments meant that design changes became prohibitively expensive much sooner in the development process. When first adopted for software development, there were no recognised alternatives for knowledge-based creative work.

Source: Wikipedia.

List of Figures

Figure 1 – Disruption by industry 3
Figure 2 – The 4th industrial revolution 18
Figure 3 – Azure Service Map 27
Figure 4 – Agile funding models 36
Figure 5 – SAFe® Portfolio Configuration ©
scaledagileframework.com 39
Figure 6 – Guiding principles for IT Strategy 78
 Figure 7 – Bimodal IT © Gartner Inc 83
Figure 8 – Cloud Maturity Model 84
Figure 9 – ITIL Service Map 97
Figure 10 – Traditional SIAM Service Model ©
www.itforbusiness.org 98
Figure 11 – Traditional vs Agile IT 101
Figure 12 – Traditional support model 104
Figure 13 – SaaS support model 104
Figure 14 – Traditional application support model 105
Figure 15 – Next generation applications support 106
Figure 16 – Azure security model 113
Figure 17 – Azure role-based access hierarchy 114
Figure 18 – Trust and control model 115
Figure 19 – Azure ExpressRoute conceptual diagram 116
Figure 20 – Monitoring map 127
Figure 21 – The DevOps problem statement 135
Figure 22 – The first, second and third way of communications .144
Figure 23 – A typical DevOps pipeline 145
Figure 24 – Azure Application Insights 147

Getting Involved

The Smart Questions community

There may be questions that we should have asked but didn't. Or specific questions which may be relevant to your situation, but not everyone in general. Go to the website for the book and post the questions. You never know, they may make it into the next edition of the book. That is a key part of the Smart Questions Philosophy.

Send us your feedback

We love feedback. We prefer great reviews, but we'll accept anything that helps take the ideas further. We welcome your comments on this book.

We'd prefer email, as it's easy to answer and saves trees. If the ideas worked for you, we'd love to hear your success stories. Maybe we could turn them into 'Talking Heads'-style video or audio interviews on our website, so others can learn from you. That's one of the reasons why we wrote this book. So talk to us.

feedback@smart-questions.com

Got a book you need to write?

Maybe you are a domain expert with knowledge locked up inside you. You'd love to share it and there are people out there desperate for your insights. But you don't think you are an author and don't know where to start. Making it easy for you to write a book is part of the Smart Questions Philosophy.

Let us know about your book idea, and let's see if we can help you get your name in print.

potentialauthor@Smart-Questions.com

Notes pages

We hope that this book has inspired you and that you have already scribbled your thoughts all over it. However if you have ideas that need a little more space then please use these notes pages.

Notes pages

Lightning Source UK Ltd.
Milton Keynes UK
UKHW02f1451171018
330708UK00003B/31/P